TREASURE ISLAND

AN ADAPTED CLASSIC

TREASURE ISLAND

ROBERT LOUIS STEVENSON

GLOBE FEARON
Pearson Learning Group

M. GEORGIA LIVINGSTON

formerly head of the English Department
Morgan Park High School
Chicago, Illinois

BESSIE C. STENHOUSE

formerly head of the English Department
Calumet High School
Chicago, Illinois

M. JERRY WEISS

Distinguished Service Professor of Communication
Jersey City State College
Jersey City, New Jersey

Cover design: Marek Antoniak
Cover illustration: Michael Garland
Text illustrations: Nathan Cabot Hale

ISBN 0-8359-0234-X
Printed in the United States of America

20 19 18 17 16   09 08 07 06

Globe
Fearon

Pearson Learning Group

1-800-321-3106
www.pearsonlearning.com

About The Author

Robert Louis Stevenson was born over a hundred years ago in Scotland. All through his childhood Stevenson was sick and could not attend school regularly. But bad health did not affect Stevenson's high spirits. In college he was known as a wild young man who refused to cut his long hair and wore velvet jackets. He became familiar with Edinburgh's underworld and used his colorful experiences there in his writings.

After college Stevenson traveled from one European health resort to another in search of a cure for his tuberculosis. In Paris he met an older American woman and fell in love with her. When she returned to America he followed. After divorcing her husband, she married Stevenson—despite the scandal.

Stevenson wrote *Treasure Island* for his wife's son. Cooped up in an English cottage, Stevenson drew a map of an imaginary island— Treasure Island—to amuse his stepson. Stevenson became fascinated by the map he had drawn. He carefully studied the shape of the island—the two harbors, the mountains. Then the idea for an adventure story came to him and he quickly outlined a series of chapters.

Treasure Island was Stevenson's first popular success. He followed this with the classic book of poetry for young people, *A Child's Garden of Verses*. After that his next book was the tale of a man with two personalities, *The Strange Case of Dr. Jekyll and Mr. Hyde.* Stevenson was now an established author. His health had improved after a stay at a resort in New York State and he decided to travel. With his wife and stepson, he sailed from San Francisco on a voyage to the South Seas (islands in the South Pacific).

Stevenson traveled in the South Seas for over a year before deciding to live there. The gentle climate and friendly people of Samoa charmed him. He decided to buy land there. Stevenson admired the native people. He wrote a book criticizing the way Europeans had treated the Samoans. Because of this book Stevenson became very popular with the native people. The Samoans called him *Tusitale,* meaning "teller of tales."

Stevenson lived for five years on Samoa until his death at the age of 44. Despite his brief life he published many excellent novels, stories, and poems. After Stevenson died the native people learned of his desire to be buried on top of a mountain "under the wide and starry sky." The native people cleared a path through the jungle to a mountain top so that Stevenson would have his wish.

Preface

The discovery of the New World brought great riches to Spain. Spanish soldiers plundered the Indian empires and then sent their loot home by boat. These Spanish treasure boats were tempting prizes for sailors of other countries. Because England was Spain's traditional enemy, English sailors were encouraged by their rulers to raid Spanish ships. The English raiders, called "Sea Dogs," were not considered pirates; they were thought of as adventurers who gave the king or queen a portion of any prize they captured.

In time, England and Spain made peace. The English were no longer allowed to attack Spanish ships. Ships were laid up and crews discharged. Many English sailors were unable to find work and they had to return to the sea as pirates. These angry sailors raided the ships of any nation. The "Golden Age of Piracy" had begun.

Piracy had great appeal for many sailors. Besides offering the chance to make a quick fortune, life aboard a pirate ship was much freer than life in the British Royal Navy. Most pirate ships operated under the rules of a written constitution. Before each voyage, the crew would draw up and sign this document listing the rules of shipboard life and the punishments for violating these rules. Pirate captains were elected by their crews and could be replaced by them. In the British Royal Navy the captains had total control over their crews. But a pirate captain had to keep his crew's favor or risk losing the position.

Pirates went to sea "on account," which meant that each pirate was a shareholder in the ship's company. The pirates' fortunes depended on the ships they raided. The saying "No prey, no pay" summed up the situation.

Most pirates were either captured or forced to give up their profession by the early 1800s. But as their strength declined, tales about pirates grew. One popularly held belief is that pirates buried great treasures. Some pirates did in fact bury their treasures, but not many. Pirates generally spent their prize money in the nearest port. With such an uncertain life, pirates were determined to live only for the moment.

CONTENTS

Book 1

The Old Captain

1 The Old Sea Dog at the "Admiral Benbow"

Squire Trelawney, Dr. Livesey, and the rest of these gentlemen have asked me to write down the whole story about Treasure Island, from the beginning to the end, keeping nothing back except how to find the island, and that only because there is still some treasure there. Accordingly, I take up my pen in the year of grace 17—, and go back to the time when my father kept the "Admiral Benbow" inn, and the brown old seaman with the sword cut first took up his lodging under our roof.

I remember him as if it were yesterday, as he came walking up to the inn door, his sea chest following behind him in a cart; a tall, strong, heavy, nut-brown man; his pigtail* falling over the shoulders of his soiled blue coat; his hands ragged and rough, with black, broken nails; and the sword cut across one cheek, a dirty white. I remember him looking round the bay and whistling to himself as he did so, and then breaking out in that old sea song that he sang so often afterward:

> "Fifteen men on the dead man's chest—
> Yo-ho-ho, and a bottle of rum!"

—in a high, old shaking voice. Then he rapped on the door with a bit of stick that he carried, and when my father appeared, called roughly for a glass of rum. This,

---

* Pigtail: the common sailor wore his hair in a short braid at the back.

when it was brought to him, he drank slowly, still looking about him at the cliffs and up at our signboard.

"This is a handy bay," says he, at length; "and a pleasant spot for an inn. Much company, mate?"*

My father told him no, very little company, the more was the pity.

"Well, then," said he, "this is the inn for me. Here you, mate," he cried to the man who wheeled the sea chest, "bring up alongside and help me get my chest up. I'll stay here a bit," he continued. "I'm a plain man; rum and bacon and eggs is what I want, and that cliff up there where I can watch for ships. What might you call me? You might call me captain. Oh, I see what you want—there!" And he threw down three or four gold pieces on the floor. "You can tell me when I've worked through that," says he, looking as fierce as a commander.

The man who came with the sea chest told us that the old seaman had asked questions about the inns that were along the coast, and hearing ours was a good inn but lonely, had chosen it for his lodgings. And that was all we could learn of our guest.

He was a very silent man by custom. All day he hung round the bay or upon the cliffs, with a brass telescope. All evening he sat in a corner of the parlor next the fire, and drank rum and water very strong. Mostly he would not speak when spoken to; only look up sudden and fierce and blow through his nose like a foghorn. And we and the people who came about our house soon learned to let him be. Every day, when he came back from his walk, he would ask if any seamen had gone by along the road. At first we thought it was

* Mate: an officer on a ship ranking below the captain.

the lack of sailor friends that made him ask this question, but at last we began to see he wished to avoid them. When a seaman put up at the "Admiral Benbow" (as now and then some did), he would look in at him through the curtained door before he entered the parlor. He was always sure to be as silent as a mouse when any such was present. For me, at least, there was no secret about the matter; for I, in a way, shared in his alarms. He had taken me aside one day, and promised me a silver fourpenny* on the first of every month if I would only keep my "weather eye open for a seaman with one leg," and let him know the moment he appeared. Often enough, when the first of the month came round, and I asked him for my pay, he would only blow through his nose at me and stare me down. But before the week was out he was sure to think better of it, bring me my fourpenny piece, and tell me again to look out for "the seaman with one leg."

How that "one-legged seaman" haunted my dreams, I need scarcely tell you. On stormy nights, when the wind shook the four corners of the house, and the sea roared along the bay and up the cliffs, I would see him in a thousand forms, and with a thousand horrible expressions. Altogether I paid pretty dear for my fourpenny piece, in the shape of these terrible dreams.

But though I was so terrified by the idea of the seaman with one leg, I was far less afraid of the captain himself than anybody else who knew him. There were nights when he took a good deal more rum and water than his head would carry. Then he would sometimes sit and sing his wicked, old, wild, sea songs, noticing

*Fourpenny: a British unit of money equal to about 14 U.S. cents when this story was written.

nobody. Sometimes he would call for glasses for everyone, and force all the trembling company to listen to his stories or sing a chorus to his songs. Often I have heard the house shaking with "Yo-ho-ho and a bottle of rum," all the neighbors joining in for dear life, with the fear of death upon them, and each singing louder than the other, hoping not to be noticed. Sometimes he would slap his hand on the table for silence all round. He would fly up in anger at a question; or sometimes because none was asked, and he thought the company was not following his story. Nor would he allow anyone to leave the inn till he had drunk himself sleepy, and had gone up to bed.

His stories were what frightened people worst of all. Dreadful stories they were; about hanging and storms at sea, and wild deeds, and strange places on the ocean. By his own story he must have lived his life among some of the most wicked men that God ever allowed upon the sea. The language in which he told these stories shocked our plain country people almost as much as the crimes that he described. My father was always saying the inn would be ruined, for people would soon stop coming there to be frightened and sent shivering to their beds. But I really believe his presence did us good. People were frightened at the time, but on looking back they rather liked it. It was a fine excitement in a quiet country life. There was even a party of the younger men who pretended to admire him, calling him a "true sea dog," and a "real old salt,"* and such names.

In one way, indeed, it seemed he would ruin us. For he kept on staying week after week, and at last month after month, so that all the money had been

* Old Salt: a man who has sailed the sea for many years.

long used up and still my father never had the courage to ask for more. If ever he mentioned it, the captain blew through his nose so loudly that you might say he roared, and stared my poor father out of the room. I am sure the terror he lived in must have greatly hastened his early and unhappy death.

All the time he lived with us the captain made no change in his dress except to buy some stockings. Part of his hat fell down, and he let it hang from that day forth. I remember the look of his coat, which he patched himself upstairs in his room, and which, before the end, was nothing but patches. He never wrote or received a letter, and he never spoke with any but the neighbors, and with these, for the most part, only when drunk on rum. The great sea chest none of us had ever seen open.

He was only once defeated, and that was toward the end, when my poor father was far gone in the illness that caused his death. Dr. Livesey came late one afternoon to see the patient. He took a bit of dinner from my mother, and went into the parlor to smoke a pipe until his horse should come down from the village, for we had no stable at the old "Benbow." I followed him in, and I remember noticing how much nicer the doctor looked, with his powdered wig as white as snow, and his bright, black eyes and pleasant manners, than the country folk, especially that dirty, heavy, pirate of ours, sitting far gone in rum, with his arms on the table. Suddenly he—the captain, that is—began to pipe up his eternal song:

> "Fifteen men on the dead man's chest—
> Yo-ho-ho, and a bottle of rum!
> Drink and the devil had done for the rest—
> Yo-ho-ho, and a bottle of rum!"

At first I had supposed "the dead man's chest" to be that big box of his upstairs in the front room, and the thought had been mixed in my dreams with that of the one-legged seaman. But by this time we had all long ceased to pay any particular notice to the song. It was new, that night, to nobody but Dr. Livesey, and on him I saw that it did not make a good impression. For he looked up for a moment quite angrily before he went on with his talk with old Taylor. In the meantime, the captain gradually brightened up at his own music, and at last flapped his hand upon the table before him in a way we all knew to mean—silence. The voices stopped at once, all but Dr. Livesey's. He went on as before, speaking clear and kind, and drawing rapidly at his pipe between every word or two. The captain glared at him for a while, flapped his hand again, glared still harder, and at last broke out with a low oath, "Silence, there, between decks!"

"Were you speaking to me, sir?" said the doctor. The pirate told him, with another oath, that this was so. "I have only one thing to say to you, sir," replied the doctor, "that if you keep on drinking rum, the world will soon be rid of a very dirty rascal!"

The old fellow's fury was awful. He sprang to his feet, drew and opened a sailor's knife, and, balancing it open on the palm of his hand, threatened to pin the doctor to the wall.

The doctor never so much as moved. He spoke to him, as before, over his shoulder, and in the same tone of voice—rather high, so that all in the room might hear, but perfectly calm and steady:

"If you do not put that knife this instant in your pocket, I promise, upon my honor, you shall hang for it."

Then followed a battle of looks between them. But the captain soon gave in, put away his weapon, and sat down grumbling like a beaten dog.

"And now, sir," continued the doctor, "since I now know there's such a fellow in my district, you may count on it, I'll have an eye upon you day and night. I'm not a doctor only; I'm an officer of the law, too. So if anyone complains about you, I'll take prompt means to have you hunted down and sent away from this place. Let that warn you."

Soon after, Dr. Livesey's horse came to the door, and he rode away. But the captain kept quiet that evening, and for many evenings to come.

2 Black Dog Appears and Disappears

It was not very long after this that there happened the first of the mysterious events that rid us at last of the captain though not, as you will see, of his affairs. It was a bitter cold winter, with long, hard frosts and heavy winds. It was plain from the first that my poor father was likely not to see the spring. He sank daily, and my mother and I had all the inn upon our hands; and were kept busy enough, without paying much attention to our rude guest.

It was one January morning, very early—a pinching, frosty morning. The bay was all gray with frost, the ripple sounding softly on the stones, the sun still low and only touching the hilltops. The captain had risen earlier than usual, and set out down the beach, his cutlass* swinging under the broad skirts of the old blue coat, his brass telescope under his arm, his hat on the back of his head. I remember his breath hanging in the air behind him like smoke as he walked off. The last sound I heard of him, as he rounded the big rock, was a loud snort as though his mind was still upon Dr. Livesey.

Well, mother was upstairs with father. I was setting the breakfast table, when the parlor door opened, and a man stepped in on whom I had never set my eyes before. He was a pale creature, with two fingers of the left hand missing. Though he wore a cutlass, he did not look much like a fighter. I always had my eye open

---

*Cutlass: a short, heavy sword, often used by sailors.

for seamen, with one leg or two, and I remember this one puzzled me. He was not a sailor, and yet he had an air of the sea about him too.

I asked him what he wished, and he said he would take rum; but as I was going out of the room to get it, he sat down upon a table and signed to me to draw near.

"Come here, sonny," says he. "Come nearer here."

I took a step nearer.

"Is this here table for my mate Bill?" he asked.

I told him I did not know his mate Bill; and this was for a person who stayed in our house, whom we called the captain.

"Well," said he, "my mate Bill would be called the captain, as like as not. He has a cut on one cheek, and a mighty pleasant way with him, especially in drink, has my mate Bill. We'll say that your captain has a cut on one cheek—the right one. Ah, well! I told you so! Now, is my mate Bill in this here house?"

I told him he was out walking.

"Which way, sonny? Which way is he gone?" And when I had pointed out the rock and told him how the captain was likely to return, and how soon, and answered a few other questions, "Ah," said he, "this'll be as good as drink to my mate Bill."

The look on his face as he said these words was not at all pleasant, but it was no business of mine, I thought; and, besides, it was difficult to know what to do. The stranger kept hanging about just inside the inn door, peering round the corner like a cat waiting for a mouse. Once I stepped out myself into the road, but he immediately called me back. As I did not obey quick enough, a most horrible change came over his face, and he ordered me in, with an oath that made me jump. As soon as I was back again he returned to his former manner, patted me on the shoulder, told me I was a good boy, and he had taken quite a liking for me. "I have a son of my own," said he, "as like you as two blocks, and he's all the pride of my heart. But the great thing for boys is to obey, sonny—to obey. Now, if you had sailed along with Bill, you wouldn't have stood there to be spoke to twice—not you. That was never Bill's way, nor the way of any that sailed with him. And here, sure enough is my mate Bill, with a telescope under his arm, bless his old heart, to be sure. You and me'll just go back into the parlor, sonny, and get behind the door, and we'll give Bill a little surprise— bless his heart, I say again."

So saying, the stranger backed along with me into the parlor, and put me behind him in the corner, so that we were both hidden by the open door. I was very uneasy and alarmed, and it added to my fears to notice that the stranger was certainly frightened himself. He cleared the handle of his cutlass and loosened the blade in its case. All the time we were waiting there he kept swallowing as if he felt a lump in his throat.

At last in walked the captain, closed the door behind him without looking to the right or left, and marched straight across the room to where his breakfast awaited him.

"Bill," said the stranger, in a voice that I thought he had tried to make bold and big.

The captain spun round on his heel and faced us. All the brown had gone out of his face, and even his nose was blue. He had the look of a man who sees a ghost. Upon my word, I felt sorry to see him, all in a moment, turn so old and sick.

"Come, Bill, you know me. You know an old shipmate, Bill, surely," said the stranger.

The captain made a sort of gasp.

"Black Dog!" said he.

"And who else?" returned the other, getting more
at his ease. "Black Dog, come for to see his old shipmate Billy, at the 'Admiral Benbow' inn. Ah, Bill, Bill,
we have seen a sight of times, us two, since I lost them
two fingers," holding up his hand.

"Now, look here," said the captain, "you've run me
down. Here I am. Well, then, speak up. What is it?"

"That's you, Bill," returned Black Dog. "You're
right, Billy. I'll have a glass of rum from this dear child
here, as I've took such a liking to; and we'll sit down, if
you please, and talk, like old shipmates."

When I returned with the rum, they were already
seated on either side of the captain's breakfast table.
Black Dog was sitting sideways and next to the door, so
as to have one eye on his old shipmate, and one, as I
thought, on the door.

He told me to go, and leave the door wide open. I
left them together and went into the bar.

For a long time, though I certainly did my best to
listen, I could hear nothing but a low murmur. But at
last the voices began to grow higher, and I could pick
up a word or two, mostly oaths, from the captain.

"No, no, no, no; and an end of it!" he cried once.
And again, "If it comes to hanging, hang all of us,
say I."

Then all of a sudden there was a tremendous burst
of oaths and other noises. The chair and table went
over in a lump. There was a cry of pain. The next
instant I saw Black Dog in full flight, and the captain

hotly pursuing, both with drawn cutlasses, and Black Dog streaming blood from the left shoulder. Just at the door, the captain aimed at Black Dog one last mighty cut. This would certainly have split him in two had it not been that the cutlass struck our big signboard of "Admiral Benbow." You may see the notch on the lower side of the frame to this day.

That blow was the last of the battle. Once out upon the road, Black Dog, in spite of his wound, disappeared over the edge of the hill in half a minute. The captain, for his part, stood staring at the signboard. Then he passed his hand over his eyes several times, and at last turned back into the house.

"Jim," says he, "rum." As he spoke, he swayed a little, and caught himself with one hand against the wall.

"Are you hurt?" I cried.

"Rum," he repeated. "I must get away from here. Rum! Rum!"

I ran to fetch it, but I was quite shaken by all that had happened, and I broke a glass. While I was still getting in my own way, I heard a loud fall in the parlor. Running in, I saw the captain lying full length upon the floor. At the same instant my mother, alarmed by the cries and fighting, came running downstairs to help me. Between us we raised his head. He was breathing very loud and hard; but his eyes were closed, and his face a horrible color.

"Dear, deary me," cried my mother, "what a shame upon the house! And your poor father sick!"

In the meantime, we had no idea what to do to help the captain, nor any other thought except that he had gotten badly hurt in the struggle with the stranger. I got the rum, to be sure, and tried to put it down his throat. But his teeth were tightly shut, and his jaws as strong as iron. It was a happy relief for us when the door opened and Dr. Livesey came in, on his visit to my father.

"Oh, doctor," we cried, "what shall we do? Where is he wounded?"

"Wounded? Fiddlesticks!" said the doctor. "No more wounded than you or I. The man has had a stroke, as I warned him. Now, Mrs. Hawkins, just you run upstairs to your husband, and tell him nothing about this. For my part, I must do my best to save this fellow's useless life. Jim here will get me a basin."

When I got back with the basin, the doctor had already torn the captain's sleeve, showing his great strong arm. A number of words and some pictures had been drawn on his skin. *"Here's luck,"* *"A fair wind,"* and *"Billy Bones,"* were on the arm. Up near the shoulder was a picture of a man hanging at the end of a rope.

"And now, Master Billy Bones, if that be your name, we'll have a look at the color of your blood. Jim," he said, "are you afraid of blood?"

"No, sir," said I.

"Well, then," said he, "you hold the basin." With that he took a knife and opened a vein.

A great deal of blood was taken before the captain opened his eyes and looked dimly about him. First he saw the doctor and frowned. Then his glance fell upon me, and he looked relieved. But suddenly his color changed, and he tried to raise himself, crying:

"Where's Black Dog?"

"There is no Black Dog here," said the doctor. "You have been drinking rum. You have had a stroke, exactly as I told you; and I have just, very much against my own will, dragged you out of the grave. Now, Mr. Bones—"

"That's not my name," he interrupted.

"Much I care," returned the doctor. "I shall call you by that name, anyway. What I have to say to you is this: one glass of rum won't kill you, but if you take one, you'll take another and another, and if you don't stop drinking right away, you'll die. Do you understand that? Die! Come now, try. Try and I'll help you to your bed."

Between us, with much trouble, we got him upstairs, and laid him on his bed, where his head fell back on the pillow, as if he were almost fainting.

"Now, mind you," said the doctor, "drinking rum is death for you."

And with that he went off to see my father, taking me with him by the arm.

"This is nothing," he said, as soon as he had closed the door. "I have drawn blood enough to keep him quiet awhile. He should lie for a week where he is— that is the best thing for him and you. But another stroke would settle him."

3 *The Black Spot*

About noon I stopped at the captain's door with some cooling drinks and medicines. He was lying very much as we had left him, only a little higher. He seemed both weak and excited.

"Jim," he said, "you're the only one here that's worth anything. And you know I've been always good to you. Never a month but I've given you a silver fourpenny for yourself. And now you see, mate, I'm pretty low, and deserted by all. Jim, you'll bring me one glass of rum, now, won't you, matey?"

"The doctor—" I began.

But he broke in cursing the doctor in a feeble but hearty voice. "Doctors is all fools," he said. That doctor there, why, what do he know about seamen? I been in places hot as fire, and mates dropping round with yellow fever, and the land rolling like the sea with earthquakes. What do the doctor know of lands like that? And I *lived* on rum, I tell you. It's been meat and drink to me. If I'm not to have my rum now, I'll die, Jim, and it will be your fault, and that doctor's." He ran on again for a while with curses. "Look, Jim, how my fingers shake," he continued, in a pleading tone. "I can't keep them still, not I. I haven't had a drop this whole day. That doctor's a fool, I tell you. If I don't have a drink of rum, Jim, I'll have the horrors. I seen some already. I seen old Cap'n Flint in the corner there behind you. As plain as print, I seen him. If I get the horrors, I'm a man that has lived rough, and I'll be sure to make trouble. Your doctor hisself said one glass wouldn't hurt me. I'll give you a golden coin for a glass, Jim."

He was growing more and more excited, and this alarmed me, for my father, who was very low that day, needed quiet. Besides, I was rather offended by the offer of money.

"I want none of your money," said I, "except what you owe my father. I'll get you one glass and no more."

When I brought it to him he seized it and drank all of it.

"Ay, ay," said he, "that's some better, sure enough. And now, mate, did that doctor say how long I was to lie here in this bed?"

"A week at least," said I.

"Thunder!" he cried. "A week! I can't do that! They'd have the black spot on me by then. The rascals are plotting against me this very moment. They couldn't keep what they got, and want to steal what is mine. I'm a saving soul. I never wasted good money of mine, nor lost it neither; and I'll trick them again. I'm not afraid of them. I'll outwit them again."

As he was thus speaking, he had risen from the bed with great difficulty, holding to my shoulder, and moving his legs like so much dead weight. His words, lively as they were in meaning, were spoken in a weak voice. He paused when he had gotten into a sitting position on the edge.

"The doctor's done me," he murmured. "My ears is singing. Lay me back."

Before I could do much to help him he had fallen back again to his former place, where he lay for a while silent.

"Jim," he said, at length, "you saw that seaman today?"

"Black Dog?" I asked.

"Ah! Black Dog," says he. "He's a bad one, but there's worse that sent him. Now, if I can't get away, and they tip me the black spot, it's my old sea chest they're after. You get on a horse—you can ride can't you? Well, then, you get on a horse, and go to that doctor. Tell him to bring the police to the 'Admiral Benbow' and they will catch all of them—all old Cap'n Flint's crew, man and boy, all of them that's left. I was first mate,* I was, old Flint's first mate, and I'm the only one that knows the place. He gave me the chart at Savannah, when he lay a-dying. But you won't tell unless they get the black spot on me, or unless you see that Black Dog again, or a seaman with one leg Jim—him above all."

"But what is the black spot, captain?" I asked.

"That's a warning, mate. I'll tell you if they get that to me. But you keep your weather eye open, Jim, and I'll share with you equals, upon my honor."

He wandered a little longer, his voice growing weaker. But soon after I had given him his medicine, which he took like a child, he fell at last into a heavy sleep in which I left him. What I should have done if all had gone well I do not know. Probably I should have told the whole story to the doctor. For I was in deadly fear lest the captain should regret having told me his story, and make an end of me. But as it happened, my poor father died quite suddenly that evening, which put all other matters on one side. Our natural grief, the visits of the neighbors, the plans for the funeral, and all the work of the inn to be carried on in the meanwhile, kept me so

---

* First Mate: an officer on board a sailing vessel next in command to the captain.

busy that I scarcely had time to think of the captain, far less to be afraid of him.

He got downstairs next morning, to be sure, and had his meals as usual, though he ate little. He had more, I'm afraid, than his usual supply of rum, for he helped himself out of the bar, frowning and blowing through his nose, and no one dared to cross him. On the night before the funeral he was as drunk as ever, and it was shocking, in that house of mourning, to hear him singing away at his ugly old sea song. Weak as he was, we were all afraid that he might die, and the doctor was suddenly taken up with a case many miles away, and was never near the house after my father's death. I have said the captain was weak. Indeed he seemed to grow weaker rather than stronger. He climbed upstairs and downstairs, and went from the parlor to the bar and back again. Sometimes he put his nose out of doors to smell the sea, holding on to the walls as he went, and breathing hard and fast like a man on a steep mountain. He never spoke directly to me, and it is my belief he had as good as forgotten his talk with me. But his temper was more uncertain and more violent than ever. He had an alarming way now when he was drunk of drawing his cutlass and laying it before him on the table. But, with all that, he paid less attention to people, and seemed shut up in his own thoughts. At times his mind seemed to wander. Once, for instance, to our extreme wonder, he piped up a different tune, a kind of country love song that he must have learned in his youth before he had begun to follow the sea.

So things passed until, the day after the funeral, and about three o'clock of a bitter, foggy, frosty afternoon, I was standing at the door for a moment, full of sad thoughts about my father, when I saw someone drawing slowly near along the road. He was plainly blind, for he tapped before him with a stick, and wore a great green shade over his eyes and nose. He was stooped, as if with age or weakness. He wore a huge, old, ragged sea cloak with a hood, that gave him a queer shape. I never saw in my life a more dreadful looking figure. He stopped a little distance from the inn. Raising his voice in an odd singsong, he spoke to the air in front of him.

"Will any kind friend inform a poor blind man, who has lost the precious sight of his eyes—where or in what part of this country he may now be?"

"You are at the 'Admiral Benbow,' Black Hill Cove, my good man," said I.

"I hear a voice," said he—"a young voice. Will you give me your hand, my kind young friend, and lead me in?"

I held out my hand, and the horrible, soft-spoken, eyeless creature gripped it in a moment like a vise. I was so much startled that I struggled to break away. But the blind man pulled me close to him with a single sweep of his arm.

"Now boy," he said, "take me in to the captain."

"Sir," said I, "upon my word I dare not."

"Oh," he said, "that's it! Take me straight in, or I'll break your arm."

And he gave it, as he spoke, a twist that made me cry out.

"Sir," said I, "it is for yourself I mean. The captain is not what he used to be. He sits with a drawn cutlass. Another gentleman—"

"Come now, march," interrupted he. I never heard a voice so cruel, and cold, and ugly as that blind man's. It frightened me more than the pain. I began to obey him at once, walking straight in at the door and toward the parlor, where our sick old pirate was sitting. The blind man held tight to me with one iron fist, and leaned almost more of his weight on me than I could carry. "Lead me straight up to him, and when I'm in view, cry out, 'Here's a friend for you, Bill.' If you don't, I'll do this," and with that he gave me such a twist that I thought I would faint. I was so utterly terrified of the blind beggar that I forgot my terror of the captain. And as I opened the parlor door, I cried out the words he had ordered in a trembling voice.

The poor captain raised his eyes. At one look the rum went out of him, and left him staring sober. The look on his face was not so much of terror as of deathly sickness. He made a movement to rise, but I do not believe he had enough force left in his body.

"Now, Bill, sit where you are," said the beggar. "I can't see but I can hear a finger moving. Business is business. Hold out your left hand. Boy, take his left hand and bring it near to my right."

We both obeyed him to the letter. Then I saw him pass something from the hollow of the hand that held his stick into the palm of the captain's, which closed upon it instantly.

"And now that's done," said the blind man. At the words he suddenly let go of me and, with great speed, went out of the parlor and into the road. I could hear his stick go tap-tap-tapping into the distance.

It was some time before either I or the captain seemed to gather our senses. At length I let go his arm, which I was still holding, and he drew in his hand and looked sharply into the palm.

"Ten o'clock!" he cried. "Six hours. We'll fool them yet!" And he sprang to his feet.

Even as he did so, he put his hand to his throat, stood swaying for a moment. Then, with a peculiar sound, fell from his whole height, face down on the floor.

I ran to him at once, calling to my mother. But haste was all in vain. The captain had been struck dead by a stroke. It is a curious thing to understand, for I had certainly never liked the man, though of late I had begun to pity him, but as soon as I saw that he was dead, I burst into a flood of tears.

4 *The Sea Chest*

I lost no time, of course, in telling my mother all that I knew. We saw ourselves at once in a difficult and dangerous position. Some of the man's money—if he had any—was certainly due to us. But it was not likely that our captain's shipmates, above all the two seen by me, Black Dog and the blind beggar, would care to give up any of the money to pay the dead man's debts. The captain's order to mount at once and ride for Dr. Livesey would have left mother alone which was not to be thought of. Indeed, it seemed impossible for either of us to stay much longer in the house. The fall of coals in the fireplace, the very ticking of the clock, filled us with alarms. The neighborhood, to our ears, seemed filled with the sound of footsteps coming toward us. The thought of the dead body of the captain on the parlor floor, and of that horrible blind beggar waiting near at hand and ready to return, filled us with terror. There were moments when I "jumped out of my skin" for fright. Something must be done at once. We decided at last to go out together and seek help in the neighboring village. No sooner said than done. Bare-headed as we were, we ran out at once in the dark of evening and the frosty fog.

The village lay not many hundred yards away, though out of view, on the other side of the next bay. Luckily it was not in the direction the blind man had gone. We were not many minutes on the road, though we sometimes stopped to listen. But there was no unusual sound—nothing but the low sound of the waves.

It was already dark when we reached the village. I shall never forget how much I was cheered to see the yellow shine in doors and windows. But that, as it proved, was the best of the help we were likely to get. For—you would have thought men would have been ashamed of themselves—no man would consent to return with us to the "Admiral Benbow." The more we told of our troubles, the more they wished to stay in their houses. The name of Captain Flint was well enough known to some there, and carried a great deal of terror. Some of the men who had been at work in a field on the other side of the "Admiral Benbow" re-membered that they had seen several strangers on the road and one at least had seen a little fishing vessel on the bay. For that matter, anyone who was a comrade of the captain's was enough to frighten them to death. And while we could get several who were willing enough to ride to Dr. Livesey's, which lay in another direction, not one would help us to defend the inn.

My mother then made a speech. She would not, she said, lose money that belonged to her fatherless boy. "If none of the rest of you dare," she said, "Jim and I dare. Back we will go the way we came, and small thanks to you big faint-hearted men. We'll have that chest open if we die for it. And I'll thank you for that bag, Mrs. Crossley, to bring back our money in."

Of course, I said I would go with my mother, and of course they all said we were foolish. But even then not a man would go along with us. All they would do was to give me a loaded pistol and to promise to have horses ready, in case we were followed on our return. In the meantime one lad was to ride to the doctor's in search of police.

My heart was beating fast when we two set forth in the cold night upon this dangerous venture. A full moon was beginning to rise and shone redly through the upper edges of the fog. This made us hurry; for it was plain that, before we came out again, all would be as bright as day, and that we surely would be seen by any watchers. We slipped along the hedges, noiseless and swift, till, to our relief, the door of the "Admiral Benbow" had closed behind us.

I locked the door at once, and we stood for a moment in the dark to catch our breath, alone in the house with the dead captain's body. Then my mother got a candle in the bar. Holding each other's hands, we went into the parlor. He lay as we had left him, on his back, with his eyes open, and one arm stretched out.

"Draw down the blind, Jim," whispered my mother. "They might come and watch outside. And now," said she, when I had done so, "we have to get the key off *that;* and who's to touch it, I should like to know!" She gave a kind of sob as she said the words.

I went down on my knees at once. On the floor close to his hand there was a little round paper, blackened on one side. I could not doubt that this was the black spot. Taking it up, I found written on the other side in a very good clear hand, this short message: "You have till ten tonight."

"He had till ten, mother," said I. Just as I said it, our old clock began striking. This sudden noise startled us shockingly. But the news was good, for it was only six.

"Now, Jim," she said, "that key."

I felt in his pockets, one after another. A few small coins, a thimble, and some thread and big needles, a piece of pigtail tobacco bitten away at the end, his knife with the crooked handle, and a pocket compass were all that they contained. I began to despair.

"Perhaps it's round his neck," suggested my mother.

I tore open his shirt at the neck. There, sure enough, hanging to a bit of string, which I cut with his own knife, we found the key. At this, we were filled with hope, and hurried upstairs to the little room where he had slept so long, and where his box had stood since the day he came to the "Admiral Benbow."

It was like any other seaman's chest on the outside. The letter "B" was burned on the top of it with a hot iron, and the corners somewhat broken as by long rough wear.

"Give me the key," said my mother. And though the lock was very stiff, she had turned it and thrown back the lid in a twinkling.

A strong smell of tobacco and tar rose from the inside, but nothing was to be seen on the top except a suit of very good clothes, carefully brushed and folded. They had never been worn, my mother said. Under that were a number of articles—several sticks of tobacco, two pairs of very handsome pistols, a piece of bar silver, an old Spanish watch, and some other objects of little value and mostly of foreign make, a pair of compasses, and five or six curious West Indian shells. I have often wondered since why he should have carried about those shells with him in his wandering, guilty, and hunted life.

In the meantime, we found nothing of any value but the bar silver, and this was not what we wished. Underneath there was an old coat, whitened with sea salt. My mother pulled it up, and there lay before us the last things in the chest—a package tied up in oilskin,* and looking like papers, and a canvas bag that gave out, at a touch, the sound of gold.

*Oilskin: an oiled cloth used for waterproof coverings.

"I'll show these rascals that I'm an honest woman," said my mother. "I'll take the money he owes me and not a penny more. Hold Mrs. Crossley's bag." And she began to count over the amount of the captain's bill from the sailor's bag into the one I was holding.

It was a long, difficult business, for the coins were of all countries and sizes. English money was about the scarcest, and it was with this only that my mother knew how to make her count.

When we were about halfway through, I suddenly put my hand upon her arm. For I had heard in the silent, frosty air a sound that brought my heart into my mouth—the tap-tapping of the blind man's stick upon the frozen road. It drew nearer and nearer, while we sat holding our breath. Then it struck sharp on the inn door. And then we could hear the handle being turned, and the lock rattling as the wretched man tried to enter. Then there was a long time of silence both inside and out. At last the tapping began again and to our great joy, died slowly away again until it could no longer be heard.

"Mother," said I, "take all of it and let's be going." For I was sure the locked door would fill him with suspicion, and would bring the whole wasp's nest about our ears. How thankful I was that I had locked it, none could tell who had never met that terrible blind man.

But my mother, frightened as she was, would not take a cent more than the captain owed her, nor a cent less. It was not yet seven, she said, by a long way; she knew her rights and she would have them. She was still talking thus, when a little low whistle sounded a good way off upon the hill. That was enough, and more than enough, for both of us.

"I'll take what I have," she said, jumping to her feet.

"And I'll take this to square the count," said I, picking up the oilskin package.

Next moment we were both feeling our way downstairs, leaving the candle by the empty chest. The next we had opened the door and were in full flight. We had not started a moment too soon. The fog was rapidly rising. Already the moon shone quite clear on the high ground on either side. It was only at the exact bottom of the hill and round the inn door that a thin veil still hung to hide the first steps of our escape. Far less than halfway to the village, very little beyond the bottom of the hill, we must come out into the moonlight. Nor was this all; for the sound of several footsteps running came already to our ears. As we looked back we could see a lantern tossing to and fro and rapidly coming toward us.

"My dear," said my mother suddenly, "take the money and run on. I am going to faint."

This was certainly the end for both of us, I thought. We were just at the little bridge, by good fortune. I helped her to the edge of the bank, where, sure enough, she gave a sigh and fell on my shoulder. I do not know how I found the strength to do it all, and I am afraid it was roughly done; but I managed to drag her down the bank and a little way under the bridge. Farther I could not move her, for the bridge was too low to let me do more than crawl below it. So there we had to stay—my mother almost in plain sight, and both of us within hearing of the inn.

5 The Last of the Blind Man

My curiosity was stronger than my fear. For I could not remain where I was, but crept back to the bank again, from which I could see the road before our door. I was scarcely in position before my enemies began to arrive, seven or eight of them, running hard, their feet beating out of time along the road, and the man with the lantern a few steps in front. Three men ran together, hand in hand. I made out, even through the mist, that the middle man of these three was the blind beggar. The next moment his voice showed me that I was right.

"Down with the door!" he cried.

"Ay, ay, sir!" answered two or three. And a rush was made upon the "Admiral Benbow," the man with the lantern following. Then I could see them pause, and hear them talking in a lower tone, as if they were surprised to find the door open. But the pause was brief, for the blind man again gave orders. His voice sounded louder and higher, as if he were wild with eagerness and rage.

"In, in, in!" he shouted, and cursed them for their delay.

Four or five of them obeyed at once, two remaining on the road with the blind beggar. There was a pause, then a cry of surprise, and then a voice shouting from the house:

"Bill's dead!"

But the blind man swore at them again for their delay.

"Search him, some of you, and the rest of you go up and get the chest," he cried.

I could hear their feet rattling up our old stairs, so that the house must have shaken. Promptly afterward, fresh sounds of astonishment arose. The window of the captain's room was thrown open with a slam and a sound of broken glass. A man leaned out into the moonlight, head and shoulders, and spoke to the blind beggar on the road below him.

"Pew," he cried, "they've been before us. Someone's turned the chest out—bottom and top."

"Is it there?" roared Pew.

"The money's there."

The blind man cursed the money.

"The papers in Flint's handwriting, I mean," he cried.

"We don't see it here nohow," returned the man.

"Here, you men downstairs, is it on Bill?" cried the blind man again.

At that, another fellow, probably the one who had remained below to search the captain's body, came to the door of the inn. "Bill's been searched already," said he, "nothing left."

"It's these people of the inn—it's that boy. I wish I had put his eyes out!" cried the blind man, Pew. "They were here no time ago—they had the door locked when I tried it. Scatter, lads, and find them."

"Sure enough, they left their candle here," said the fellow from the window.

"Scatter and find them! Search the whole house!" repeated Pew, striking his stick upon the road.

Then there followed a great to-do through all our old inn, heavy feet pounding to and fro, furniture thrown over and doors kicked in. Next the men came out on the road again, one after another, and declared that we were not to be found. Just then the same whistle that had alarmed my mother and myself over the dead captain's money was once more clearly heard through the night, but this time twice repeated. I had thought it to be the blind man's whistle, calling his crew. Now I found that it was a signal from the hillside toward the village, and, from the way the pirates acted when they heard it, a signal to warn them of danger.

"There's Dirk again," said one. "Twice! We'll have to go, mates."

"Fools!" cried Pew. "Dirk was a coward from the first—you must not mind him. The woman and boy must be close by. They can't be far. Scatter and look for them, dogs! Oh, shiver my soul," he cried, "if only I had eyes!"

Two of the fellows began to look here and there among the lumber, but, I thought, with half an eye to their own danger all the time, while the rest stood on the road.

"You have your hands on thousands of pounds, you fools, and you hang back! You'd be as rich as kings if you could find it, and you know it's here. Yet you stand there. There wasn't one of you dared face Bill, and I did it—a blind man! And I'm to lose my chance because of you! I'm to be a poor, crawling beggar, begging for rum, when I might be rolling in a coach! If you had any pluck, you would catch them still."

"Hang it, Pew, we've got the Spanish gold!" grumbled one.

"They might have hid the papers," said another. "Take what's left, Pew, and don't stand there screaming!"

Screaming was the word for it, Pew's anger rose so high. At last he became so angry that he struck at them right and left in his blindness. His stick sounded heavily on more than one.

These, in their turn, cursed back at the blind wretch, threatened him in horrid terms, and tried in vain to catch the stick and twist it from his grasp.

This quarrel was what saved us. For while it was still going on, another sound came from the top of the hill on the side of the village—the tramp of horses galloping. Almost at the same time a pistol shot, flash and report, came from the hedge side. That was plainly the last signal of danger, for the pirates turned at once and ran, separating in every direction. One ran toward the sea along the bay, one across the hill, and so on, so that in half a minute not a sign of them remained but Pew. They deserted him and there he remained behind, tapping up and down the road in a fury, and calling for his comrades. Finally he took the wrong turn, and ran a few steps past me toward the village, crying:

"Johnny, Black Dog, Dirk," and other names, "you won't leave old Pew, mates—not old Pew!"

Just then the sound of horses galloping came over the top of the hill, and four or five riders came in sight in the moonlight, and swept at full speed down the slope.

At this Pew saw his mistake, turned with a scream, and ran straight for the ditch, into which he rolled. But he was on his feet again in a second, and made another dash, now not knowing where to go, right under the nearest of the coming horses.

The rider tried to save him, but in vain. Down went Pew with a cry that rang high into the night. The four hoofs trampled him and passed by. He fell on his side, then gently sank upon his face, and moved no more.

I leaped to my feet and hailed the riders. They were pulling up, at any rate, horrified at the accident. I soon saw who they were. One, coming up behind the rest, was the lad that had gone from the village to Dr. Livesey's. The rest were officers whom he had met by the way, and with whom he had the good sense to return at once. Some news of the fishing vessel in the bay had found its way to Mr. Dance, the chief officer, and sent him out that night in our direction. To that fact my mother and I owed our lives.

Pew was dead, stone dead. My mother, when we had carried her up to the village, was none the worse for her terror, though she still continued to wish she had taken the rest of the money. In the meantime, Mr. Dance rode on toward the bay where the fishing vessel had been seen. He was not surprised, when he and his men got down to the water's edge, to find that the vessel was already under way, though still close to shore. He hailed her. A voice replied, telling him to keep out of the moonlight or he would get some lead in him, and at the same time a bullet whistled close by his arm. Soon after, the vessel rounded the point and disappeared.

"They've got off clean, and that's the end of it. Only," he added, "I'm glad Master Pew did not get away," for by this time he had heard my story.

I went back with him to the "Admiral Benbow." You cannot imagine a house in such a state of ruin. The very clock had been thrown down by these fellows in their furious hunt after my mother and myself. Though nothing had actually been taken away except the captain's bag of money and a little silver from the till, I could see at once that we were ruined. Mr. Dance could make nothing of the scene.

"They got the money, you say? Well, then, Hawkins, what were they after? More money, I suppose?"

"No, sir, not money, I think," replied I. "In fact, sir, I believe I have the thing in my pocket. And to tell you the truth, I should like to get it put in safety."

"To be sure boy; quite right," said he. "I'll take it, if you like."

"I thought perhaps Dr. Livesey—" I began.

"Perfectly right," he interrupted, very cheerfully, "perfectly right—a gentleman and an officer. Now that I come to think of it, I might as well ride around there myself and report to him or squire. Now, I'll tell you, Hawkins; if you like, I'll take you along."

I thanked him heartily for the offer, and we walked back to the village, where the horses were. By the time I had told mother of my purpose they were all in the saddle.

"Dogger," said Mr. Dance, "you have a good horse. Take up this lad behind you."

As soon as I was mounted, holding on to Dogger's belt, Mr. Dance gave the word, and the party struck out at a trot on the road to Dr. Livesey's house.

6 *The Captain's Papers*

We rode hard all the way, till we drew up before Dr. Livesey's door. The house was all dark to the front.

Mr. Dance told me to jump down and knock. The door was opened almost at once by the maid.

"Is Dr. Livesey in?" I asked.

No, she said. He had come home in the afternoon, but had gone up to the squire's* to dine and pass the evening with him.

"So there we go, boys," said Mr. Dance.

We went to the gates, and up the long moonlit avenue to the squire's home. Here Mr. Dance got off his horse, and, taking me along with him, was let into the house.

The servant led us down a long passage, and showed us into a great library, all lined with books, where the squire and Dr. Livesey sat, pipe in hand, on either side of a bright fire.

I had never seen the squire so near at hand. He was a tall man, over six feet high, and broad as well. He had a bluff, rough-and-ready face, all roughened and reddened and lined from his long travels. His eyebrows were very black and moved often, and this gave him a look of some temper, not bad, you would say, but quick and high.

"Come in, Mr. Dance," says he.

"Good evening, Dance," says the doctor, with a nod. "And good evening to you, friend Jim. What good wind brings you here?"

*Squire: a country gentleman, especially the person who runs a district in England.

Mr. Dance stood up straight and stiff, and told his story like a lesson. You should have seen how the two gentlemen leaned forward and looked at each other, and forgot to smoke in their surprise and interest. When they heard how my mother went back to the inn, Dr. Livesey fairly slapped his leg, and the squire cried "Bravo!" and knocked the ashes from his long pipe. Long before it was done, Mr. Trelawney (that, you will remember, was the squire's name) had got up from his seat, and was walking rapidly about the room. The doctor, as if to hear better, had taken off his powdered wig, and sat there, looking very strange indeed with his own short black hair.

At last Mr. Dance finished the story.

"Mr. Dance," said the squire, "you are a very noble fellow. And as for riding down that black rascal, I think it a good deed, sir. This lad Hawkins is brave, I see. Hawkins, will you ring that bell? Mr. Dance must have some wine."

"And so, Jim," said the doctor, "you have the thing that they were after, have you?"

"Here it is, sir," said I, and gave him the oilskin package.

The doctor looked it all over, as if his fingers ached to open it. But, instead of doing that, he put it quietly in the pocket of his coat.

"Squire," said he, "when Dance has had his wine he must, of course, be off on duty; but I mean to keep Jim Hawkins here to sleep at my house. With your permission, I think we should have the servant bring up the cold pie, and let him eat."

"As you wish, Livesey," said the squire. "Hawkins has earned better than cold pie."

So a big pigeon pie was brought in and put on a side table, and I made a hearty supper, for I was as hungry as a bear. Mr. Dance was further praised, and at last dismissed.

"And now, squire," said the doctor.

"And now, Livesey," said the squire, in the same breath.

"One at a time, one at a time," laughed Dr. Livesey. "You have heard of this Flint, I suppose?"

"Heard of him!" cried the squire. "Heard of him, you say! He was feared more than any pirate that ever sailed the seas."

"Well, I've heard of Captain Flint myself," said the doctor. "But the point is, had he money?"

"Money!" cried the squire. "Have you heard Jim's story? What were these rascals after but money? What do they care for but money? For what would they risk their rascal necks but money?"

"That we shall soon know," replied the doctor. "What I want to know is this: supposing that I have here in my pocket some hint of where Flint buried his treasure, will that treasure amount to much?"

"Amount, sir!" cried the squire. "It will amount to this: if we have the hint you talk about, I shall fit out a ship in Bristol,* and take you and Hawkins here along. I'll have that treasure if I search a year."

"Very well," said the doctor. "Now, then, if Jim is agreeable, we'll open the package." And he laid it before him on the table.

The package was sewed together, and the doctor had to cut the threads to open it. It contained two things—a book and a sealed paper.

---

* Bristol: a seaport in southwest England.

"First of all we'll try the book," observed the doctor.

The squire and I were both peering over his shoulder as he opened it, for Dr. Livesey had kindly made a sign to me to come round from the side table, where I had been eating, to enjoy the sport of the search. On the first page there were only some scraps of writing, such as a man with a pen in his hand might make for idleness or practice. One was the same as the mark on the captain, "Billy Bones." There was also, "Mr. W. Bones, mate." "No more rum." "Off Palm Key he got itt," and some other bits, mostly single words that we could not make out. I could not help wondering who it was that had "got itt," and what "itt" was that he got. A knife in his back as likely as not.

"Not much to be learned there," said Dr. Livesey, as he passed on.

The next ten or twelve pages were filled with a number of curious items. There was a date at one end of the line and at the other a sum of money, as in common account books. But instead of any writing to explain each sum, only a number of crosses was between the two. On the 12th of June, 1745, for instance, a sum of 70 pounds had plainly been paid to someone, and there was nothing but six crosses to explain the cause.

The record lasted over nearly 20 years, the amount of the sums growing larger as time went on. At the end a grand total had been made out after five or six wrong additions, and these words added, "Bones, his pile."

"I can't make head or tail of this," said Dr. Livesey.

"The thing is as clear as noonday," cried the squire. "This is the black-hearted hound's account book. These crosses stand for the names of ships or towns that they sank or robbed. The sums are the rascal's share, and where he feared the account would not be clear, you see he added something clearer. 'Off Caraccas,' now. You see, here was some unhappy

vessel boarded off that coast. God help the poor souls that sailed in her—dead long ago."

"Right!" said the doctor. "Right! And the amounts increase, you see, as he rose in rank." There was little else in the book.

"And now," said the squire, "for the other."

The paper had been sealed in several places with a thimble by way of a seal. The very thimble, perhaps, that I had found in the captain's pocket. The doctor opened the seals with great care, and out fell the map of an island, with latitude and longitude, depth of the water along the coast, names of hills and bays, and every bit of information that would be needed to bring a ship to a safe harbor upon its shores. The island was about nine miles long and five across and had two fine harbors, and a hill in the center part marked "The Spyglass." There were several additions of a later date; but, above all, three crosses in red ink—two on the north part of the island, one in the southwest. Beside this last, in the same red ink, and in a small neat hand, very different from the captain's shaky handwriting, were these words: *Most of the treasure here.*

Over on the back the same hand had written this:

"Tall tree, Spyglass shoulder, bearing a point to the N. of N.N.E.

"Skeleton Island E.S.E. and by E.

"Ten feet.

"The bar silver is in the north hiding place. You can find it by the direction of the east hill, 60 feet south of the black cliff with the face on it.

"The arms are easy found, in the sand hill, N. point of north inlet cape, bearing E. and quarter N.

"J. F."

That was all. I could not understand it at all, but it filled the squire and Dr. Livesey with delight.

"Livesey," said the squire, "you will give up your work as a doctor at once. Tomorrow I start for Bristol. In three weeks' time—three weeks! Two weeks—ten days—we'll have the best ship, sir, and the choicest crew in England. Hawkins shall come as cabin boy.* You'll make a fine cabin boy, Hawkins. You, Livesey, are ship's doctor. We'll take Redruth, Joyce, and Hunter. We'll have good winds, a quick passage and not the least difficulty in finding the spot."

"Trelawney," said the doctor, "I'll go with you, and so will Jim. There's only one man I'm afraid of."

"And who's that?" cried the squire. "Name the dog, sir!"

"You," replied the doctor, "for you cannot hold your tongue. We are not the only men who know of this paper. These fellows who attacked the inn tonight—bold, desperate men, for sure—and the rest who stayed aboard that fishing vessel, and others, not far off, are bound that they'll get that money. We must none of us be alone till we get to sea. Jim and I shall stick together in the meanwhile. You'll take Joyce and Hunter when you ride to Bristol, and, from first to last, not one of us must breathe a word of what we've found."

"Livesey," returned the squire, "you are always in the right. I'll be as silent as the grave."

* Cabin Boy: a boy employed to wait on the officers and passengers in a boat or ship.

Book 2

The Sea Cook

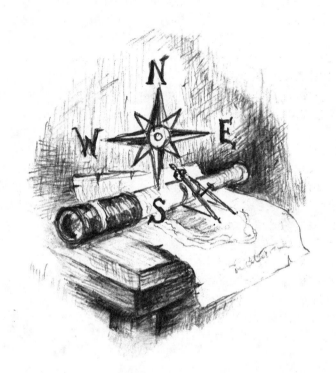

7 *I Go to Bristol*

It was longer than the squire imagined before we were ready for the sea, and none of our first plans—not even Dr. Livesey's, of keeping me beside him—could be carried out as we had planned. Doctor Livesey had to go to London for another doctor to take his place; the squire was hard at work at Bristol; and I lived on at the squire's under the care of old Redruth. I was full of thoughts of the sea and the most charming dreams of strange islands and adventures. I thought by the hour about the map, all of which I well remembered. Sitting by the fire in the housekeeper's room, I sailed to that island in my dreams, from every possible direction. I explored every acre of its surface. I climbed a thousand times to that tall hill they call the Spyglass, and from the top enjoyed the most wonderful and changing scenes. Sometimes the isle was thick with savages, with whom we fought; sometimes full of dangerous animals that hunted us. But in all my dreams nothing happened to me so strange and awful as our actual adventures.

So the weeks passed on, till one fine day there came a letter addressed to Dr. Livesey, with this addition, "To be opened, in the case of his absence, by Tom Redruth or young Hawkins." Obeying this order I found the following important news:

"*Old Anchor Inn, Bristol, March 1, 17 —*

"Dear Livesey, — As I do not know whether you are at the squire's or still in London, I send this in double to both places.

"The ship is bought and fitted. She lies at anchor, ready for sea. You never imagined a sweeter schooner* — a child might sail her — 200 tons; name, *Hispaniola.*

"I got her through my old friend, Blandly, who has proved to be most helpful. The good fellow really slaved for me, and so, I may say, did everyone in Bristol, as soon as they got news of what we are sailing for — treasure, I mean."

"Redruth," said I, interrupting the letter, "Dr. Livesey will not like that. The squire has been talking, after all."

"Well, who's a better right?" growled Redruth. "A queer thing if squire ain't to talk because of Dr. Livesey, I should think."

At that I said no more, and read straight on:

"Blandly himself found the *Hispaniola,* and got her cheap. There is a class of men in Bristol who are against Blandly. They are saying that this honest creature would do anything for money, that the *Hispaniola* belonged to him, and that he sold it to me at much too high a price — but these things are false. None of them dare, however, to deny that the ship is excellent.

"So far everything is going along well. The workmen, to be sure were slow; but time cured that. It was the crew that troubled me.

"I wanted at least 20 men in case there are savages or pirates on the island, and I could scarcely find half a dozen, till great good luck brought me the very man that I needed.

"I was standing on the dock, when, by chance, I began to talk with him. I found he was an old sailor, kept an inn, and knew all the seamen in Bristol. He had lost his health on shore, and wanted a good job as cook to get to sea again. He

* Schooner: a sailing vessel.

had hobbled down there that morning, he said, to get a smell of the salt.

"I was greatly touched—so would you have been—and, out of pure pity, I hired him on the spot to be ship's cook. Long John Silver, he is called, and has lost a leg; but that I thought in his favor, since he lost it in his country's service.

"Well, sir, I thought I had only found a cook, but it was a crew I had discovered. Between Silver and myself we got together in a few days a company of the toughest old salts you could imagine—not pretty to look at, but fellows, by their faces, of high spirit.

"Long John even got rid of two out of the six or seven I had already hired. He showed me in a moment that they were just the sort of men we had to fear in an adventure of importance.

"I am in the best of health and spirits, eating and sleeping well, yet I shall not enjoy a moment till we set out to sea. Seaward ho! Hang the treasure! It's the glory of the sea that has turned my head. So now, Livesey, quickly, do not lose an hour.

"Let Hawkins go at once to see his mother, with Redruth for a guard. Then both come full speed to Bristol.

"John Trelawney

"Postscript—I did not tell you that Blandly, who, by the way, is to send a ship after us if we don't turn up by the end of August, found a fine fellow for captain. He's a strict man, which I regret, but, in all other respects, a treasure. Long John Silver got a very capable man for a mate, a man named Arrow.

"I forgot to tell you that Silver is a man of some wealth. I know it to be true that he has a bank account. He leaves his wife to manage the inn while he is at sea.

"J. T.

"P.P.S.—Hawkins may stay one night with his mother.

"J. T."

You can imagine the excitement into which that letter put me. I was half beside myself with joy. If ever I despised a man, it was old Tom Redruth, who could do nothing but grumble and complain.

The next morning he and I set out on foot for the "Admiral Benbow," and there I found my mother in good health and spirits. The captain, who had long been a cause of so much misery, was gone. The squire had had everything repaired and the public rooms and the sign painted, and had added some furniture — above all a beautiful chair for mother in the bar. He had found her a boy as a helper also, so that she should not be without help while I was gone.

The night passed, and the next day after dinner, Redruth and I were out again and on the road. I said good-bye to mother and the bay where I had lived since I was born, and the dear old "Admiral Benbow." One of my last thoughts was of the captain, who had so often walked along the beach with his hat set on one side of his head, his sword-cut cheek, and his old brass telescope. Next moment we had turned the corner, and my home was out of sight.

The coach picked us up early in the evening. I was squeezed in between Redruth and a stout old gentleman, and in spite of the swift motion and the cold night air, I must have slept like a log. When I was awakened at last, it was by a push in the ribs. I opened my eyes to find that we were standing still before a large building in a city street, and that it was broad daylight.

"Where are we?" I asked.

"Bristol," said Tom. "Get down."

Mr. Trelawney was staying at an inn far down the docks, to take charge of the work upon the schooner.

We now walked toward it, and our way, to my great delight, lay along the docks and beside great numbers of ships of all sizes and nations. In one, sailors were singing at their work. In another, there were men working on the mast, high over my head, hanging to ropes that seemed no thicker than a spider's web. Though I had lived by the shore all my life, I seemed never to have been near the sea till then. The smell of tar and salt was something new. I saw many old sailors with rings in their ears, and curled whiskers, and pigtails; and watched their rolling, clumsy sea walk. I could not have been more delighted.

And I was going to sea myself; to sea in a schooner, with pigtailed singing seamen; to sea, bound for an unknown island, to seek for buried treasures!

While I was still in this delightful dream, we came suddenly in front of a large inn and met Squire Trelawney, all dressed out like a sea officer, in stout blue cloth. He was coming out of the door with a smile on his face, and an excellent imitation of a sailor's walk.

"Here you are," he cried, "and the doctor came last night from London. Bravo! The ship's company is complete!"

"Oh, sir," cried I, "when do we sail?"

"Sail!" says he. "We sail tomorrow!"

8

At the Sign of the "Spyglass"

When I had finished breakfast the squire gave me a note addressed to John Silver, at the sign of the "Spyglass," and told me I should easily find the place by following the line of the docks, and keeping a bright look out for a little inn with a large brass telescope for a sign. I set off, happy at this chance to see some more of the ships and seamen. I picked my way among a great crowd of people and carts and boxes, for the dock was now at its busiest, until I found the inn.

It was a bright enough little place. The sign was newly painted; the windows had neat red curtains; the floor was covered with clean sand. There was a street on either side and an open door on both, which made the large low room pretty clear to see in, in spite of clouds of tobacco smoke.

The customers were mostly seamen. They talked so loudly that I hung at the door, almost afraid to enter.

As I was waiting, a man came out of a side room and, at a glance, I was sure he must be Long John. One of his legs was cut off close by the hip, and under his shoulder he carried a crutch, which he managed with wonderful skill, hopping about upon it like a bird. He was very tall and strong, with a face as big as a ham—plain and pale, but intelligent and smiling. Indeed, he seemed in the most cheerful spirits, whistling as he moved about among the tables, with a merry word or a slap on the shoulder for his favorite guests.

Now, to tell you the truth, from the very first mention of Long John in Squire Trelawney's letter, I had been afraid that he might prove to be the very one-legged sailor whom I had watched for so long at the old "Benbow." But one look at the man before me was enough. I had seen the captain and Black Dog and the blind man Pew, and I believed I knew what a pirate was like—a very different creature, I thought, from this clean and pleasant-tempered landlord.

I gathered courage at once and walked right up to the man where he stood propped on his crutch, talking to a seaman.

"Mr. Silver, sir?" I asked, holding out the note.

"Yes, my lad," said he. "Such is my name, to be sure. And who may you be?" And then as he saw the squire's letter, he seemed to me to give something almost like a jump.

"Oh!" said he, quite loud, and holding out his hand, "I see. You are our new cabin boy. Pleased I am to see you."

And he took my hand in his large firm grasp.

Just then one of the customers at the far side rose suddenly and made for the door. He was out in the street in a moment. But his hurry had made me notice him and I knew him at a glance. It was the white-faced man, with two fingers missing, who had come first to the "Admiral Benbow."

"Oh," I cried, "stop him! It's Black Dog!"

"I don't care two cents who he is," cried Silver. "But he hasn't paid his bill. Harry, run and catch him."

One of the others who was nearest the door leaped up and started after him.

"Even if he were Admiral Hawke he shall pay his bill," cried Silver. Then letting go my hand—"Who did you say he was?" he asked. "Black what?"

"Dog, sir," said I. "Has Mr. Trelawney not told you of the pirates? He was one of them."

"So?" cried Silver. "In my house! Ben, run and help Harry. One of those rascals, was he? Was that you drinking with him, Morgan? Step up here."

The man whom he called Morgan—an old gray-haired, red-faced sailor—came forward with an awkward walk, rolling his tobacco in his mouth.

"Now, Morgan," said Long John, very sternly; "you never clapped eyes on that Black—Black Dog before, did you, now?"

"Not I, sir," said Morgan, with a salute.

"You didn't know his name, did you?"

"No, sir."

"By the powers,* Tom Morgan, it's a good thing for

* "By the Powers!": sailor's exclamation.

you that you don't!" exclaimed the landlord. "If you had been mixed up with the like of that, you would never have put another foot in my house, you may lay to that.* And what was he saying to you?"

"I don't rightly know, sir," answered Morgan.

"Do you call that a head on your shoulders?" cried Long John. "Don't rightly know, don't you! Perhaps you don't happen to rightly know who you was speaking to, perhaps? Get back to your place, Tom."

And then, as Morgan rolled back to his seat, Silver added to me in a whisper that was very flattering, as I thought:

"He's quite an honest man, Tom Morgan, only stupid. And now," he ran on again, aloud, "let's see— Black Dog? No, I don't know the name, not I. Yet I kind of think I've—yes, I've seen the rascal. He used to come here with a blind beggar, he used."

"That he did, you may be sure," said I. "I knew that blind man, too. His name was Pew."

"It was!" cried Silver, now quite excited. "Pew! That were his name all right. Ah, he looked like a rascal, he did! If we catch this Black Dog, now, that will be good news for Cap'n Trelawney! Ben's a good runner. Few seamen run better than Ben. He should catch him, by the powers!"

All the time he was jerking out these words he was stumping up and down the inn on his crutch, slapping tables with his hand, and acting so excited that anyone would have believed him. My suspicions had returned when I saw Black Dog at the "Spyglass," and I watched Silver closely. But he was too deep, and too ready, and too clever for me. By the time the two men had come back out of breath, and said that they had

* "You May Lay to That!": sailor's exclamation.

lost track of Black Dog in a crowd, and had been scolded, I was sure of the honesty of Long John Silver.

"See here now, Hawkins," said he, "this is a hard thing on a man like me, now ain't it? There's Cap'n Trelawney—what's he to think? Here I have this Black Dog sitting in my own house, drinking of my own rum! Here you comes and tells me of it plain; and here I let him give us all the slip before my very eyes. Now, Hawkins, you do me justice with the cap'n. You're a lad, you are, but you're as smart as paint. I see that when you first came in. But what could I do, with this old crutch I hop around on?"

And then, all of a sudden, he stopped, and his jaw dropped as though he had remembered something.

"The bill!" he burst out. "Three glasses of rum! Why, shiver my timbers,* if I hadn't forgotten the bill!"

And, falling on a bench, he laughed until the tears ran down his cheeks. I could not help joining. We laughed together until the inn rang again.

"Why, what a precious old sea calf** I am!" he said at last, wiping his cheeks. "You and me should get on well, Hawkins, for I swear I should be the ship's boy. But this won't do. Duty is duty, mates. I'll put on my old hat, and step along with you to Cap'n Trelawney and report this here affair. For, mind you, it's serious, young Hawkins; and neither you nor me has come out of it with credit. But dash my buttons! That was a good one about the bill."

And he began to laugh again so heartily that,

---

* "Shiver My Timbers!": sailor's exclamation.
** Sea Calf: a small, spotted seal, also known as a harbor seal.

though I did not see the joke as he did, I was again obliged to join him laughing.

On our little walk along the docks, he made himself the most interesting companion. He told me about the different ships that we passed by, explaining the work that was going on—how one was loading, another unloading, and a third making ready for sea. Every now and then he told me some little story of ships or seamen, or repeated a bit of seaman's language till I had learned it perfectly. I began to see that here was one of the best of possible shipmates.

When we got to the inn, the squire and Dr. Livesey were seated together, finishing a quart of ale before going aboard the schooner to look it over.

Long John told the story from first to last, with a great deal of spirit and the most perfect truth. "That was how it were, now, weren't it Hawkins?" he would say, now and again, and I could always agree.

The two gentlemen were sorry that Black Dog had got away. But we all agreed there was nothing to be done, and after he had been praised, Long John took up his crutch and left.

"All hands aboard by four this afternoon," shouted the squire after him.

"Ay, ay, sir," cried the cook.

"Well, squire," said Dr. Livesey, "I don't put much faith in your discoveries, as a general thing; but I will say this, John Silver suits me."

"The man's a perfect gem," declared the squire.

"And now," added the doctor, "Jim may come on board with us, may he not?"

"To be sure he may," says squire. "Take your hat Hawkins, and we'll see the ship."

9 Powder and Arms

The *Hispaniola* lay some way out, and we went under the bows* and round the sterns** of many other ships to get to her. At last, however, we got alongside, and were met and saluted as we stepped aboard by the mate, Mr. Arrow, a brown old sailor with rings in his ears. He and the squire were very thick and friendly, but I soon observed that things were not the same between Mr. Trelawney and the captain.

The captain was a sharp-looking man, who seemed angry with everything on board, and was soon to tell us why, for we had hardly got down into the cabin when a sailor followed us.

"Captain Smollett, sir, asking to speak with you," said he.

"I am always at the captain's orders. Show him in," said the squire.

The captain, who was close behind, entered at once and shut the door behind him.

"Well, Captain Smollett, what have you to say? All well, I hope. Everything in good shape?"

"Well, sir," said the captain, "I'd better speak plain, I believe, even at the risk of offense. I don't like this cruise; I don't like the men; and I don't like Mr. Arrow. That's short and sweet."

"Perhaps, sir, you don't like the ship?" inquired the squire, very angry, as I could see.

*Bow: the part of the ship farthest front.
**Stern: the rear of a ship.

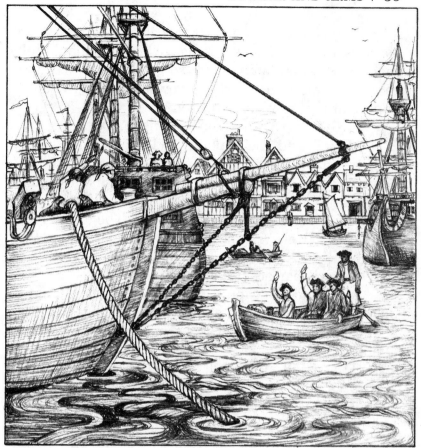

"I can't speak as to that, sir, not having seen her tried," said the captain. "She seems a clever vessel; more I can't say."

"Possibly, sir, you may not like me, either?" says the squire.

But here Dr. Livesey cut in.

"Wait a bit," said he, "wait a bit. Such questions as that make ill feeling. The captain has said too much or he has said too little, and I want an explanation of his words. You say you don't like this cruise. Now, why?"

"I was hired, sir, on what we call sealed orders,* to sail this ship for that gentleman where he should tell me," said the captain. "So far so good. But now I find that every man on the ship knows more than I do. I don't call that fair, now, do you?"

"No," said Dr. Livesey, "I don't."

"Next," said the captain, "I learn we are going after treasure—hear it from my own men, mind you. Now, treasure is dangerous work. I don't like treasure voyages on any account; and I don't like them, above all, when they are secret and when (begging your pardon, Mr. Trelawney) the secret has been told to the parrot."

"Silver's parrot?" asked the squire.

"No," said the captain. "Blabbed, I mean. It's my belief neither of you gentlemen know what you are about. But I'll tell you my way of it—life or death, and a close run."

"That is all clear and, I suppose, true enough," replied Dr. Livesey. "We take the risk; but we are not so ignorant as you believe us. Next, you say you don't like the crew. Are they not good seamen?"

"I don't like them, sir," returned Captain Smollett. "And I think I should have had the choosing of my own men."

"Perhaps you should," replied the doctor. "My friend should perhaps have taken you along with him; but the slight, if there be one, was not meant. And you don't like Mr. Arrow?"

"I don't sir. I believe he's a good seaman; but he's too free with the crew to be a good officer. A mate

---

* Sealed Orders: the captain who sails under "sealed orders" does not know where he is to go until after he is out to sea.

should keep to himself. He shouldn't drink with the seamen."

"Do you mean he drinks?" cried the squire.

"No, sir," replied the captain, "only that he's too familiar."

"Well, now, captain," said the doctor. "Tell us what you want."

"Well, gentlemen, are you determined to go on this cruise?"

"Like iron," answered the squire.

"Very good," said the captain. "Then, as you've heard me very patiently saying things that I could not prove, hear me a few words more. They are putting the powder and the arms in the front, under the seamen's rooms. Now, you have a good place under the cabin* —near the officer's rooms. Why not put them there? —first point. Then you are bringing four of your own people with you, and they tell me some of them are to be put forward with the crew. Why not give them their rooms back here beside the cabin?—second point."

"Any more?" asked Mr. Trelawney.

"One more," said the captain. "There's been too much blabbing already."

"Far too much," agreed the doctor.

"I'll tell you what I've heard myself," continued Captain Smollett: "that you have a map of an island; that there's crosses on the map to show where treasure is; and that the island lies—" And then he gave the exact directions for reaching it.

"I never told that," cried the squire, "to a soul!"

"The men know it, sir," returned the captain.

"Livesey, that must have been you or Hawkins," cried the squire.

* Cabin: the rooms toward the rear, or stern, where the officers of the ship live.

"It doesn't much matter who it was," replied the doctor. And I could see that neither he nor the captain paid much attention to Mr. Trelawney's words. Neither did I, to be sure, he was so free a talker. Yet in this case I believe he was really right, and that nobody had told where the island lay.

"Well, gentlemen," continued the captain, "I don't know who has this map, but I make it a point that it shall be kept secret even from me and Mr. Arrow. Otherwise I would ask you to get another man for captain."

"I see," said the doctor. "You wish us to keep this matter dark, and you wish all the powder and arms kept in the stern of the ship in the care of our own friends. In other words, you fear a mutiny."*

"Sir," said Captain Smollett, "no captain would be right in going to sea at all if he had a good reason for saying that. As for Mr. Arrow, I believe him thoroughly honest; some of the men are the same; all may be for what I know. But it is my duty to make sure of the ship's safety and the life of every man aboard of her. I see things going, as I think, not quite right. And I ask you to take certain steps to prevent trouble, or let me give up my position as captain. And that's all."

"Captain Smollett," said the doctor with a smile, "when you came in here, you meant more than this."

"Doctor," said the captain, "you are smart. When I came in here I meant to anger Mr. Trelawney so that he would take my position away from me. I did not think that he would listen to a word."

"And I would not," cried the squire, "if Livesey had not been here. As it is, I have heard you. I will do as you wish, but I think the worse of you."

* Mutiny: the seizing or stealing of a ship by the crew.

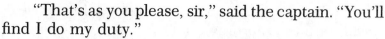

"That's as you please, sir," said the captain. "You'll find I do my duty."

And with that he took his leave.

"Trelawney," said the doctor, "contrary to all my notions, I believe you have managed to get two honest men on board with you—that man and John Silver."

"Silver, if you like," cried the squire, "but not that captain!"

"Well," says the doctor, "we shall see."

When we came on deck, the men had begun already to take out the arms and powder, yo-ho-ing at their work, while the captain and Mr. Arrow stood by looking on.

The new arrangement was quite to my liking. The whole schooner had been changed. Six rooms had been made at the rear, and this set of cabins was only joined to the front part of the ship, where the crew lived, by a long passage. It had at first been meant that the captain, Mr. Arrow, Hunter, Joyce, the doctor, and the squire were to have these six cabins. Now, Redruth and I were to get two of them, and Mr. Arrow and the captain were to sleep on deck. Even the mate seemed pleased with the arrangements. Perhaps he, too, had been doubtful as to the crew, but that is only guess. For as you shall hear, we did not long have him with us.

We were all hard at work changing the powder and the cabins, when the last man or two, and Long John along with them, came aboard.

Silver came up the side like a monkey for cleverness and, as soon as he saw what was going on, "So ho, mates!" says he, "what's this?"

"We're a-changing of the powder, Silver," answers one.

"Why, by the powers," cried Long John, "if we do, we'll miss the morning tide!"

"My orders!" said the captain shortly. "You may go below, my man. The men will want supper."

"Ay, ay, sir," answered Long John; and touching his forehead, he disappeared at once in the direction of his galley.*

"That's a good man, captain," said the doctor.

"Very likely, sir," replied Captain Smollett. "Easy with that, men—easy," he ran on, to the fellows who were shifting the powder. Then suddenly seeing me examining the big gun we carried on board the ship, he cried, "Here, you ship's boy, out of that! Off with you to the cook and get some work."

And then as I was hurrying off I heard him say, quite loudly, to the doctor:

"I'll have no favorites on my ship."

I assure you I was quite of the squire's way of thinking, and hated the captain deeply.

*Galley: ship's kitchen.

10 *The Voyage*

All that night we were very busy getting things stored in their place. Boats filled with the squire's friends, Mr. Blandly and others, came to wish him a good voyage and a safe return. We never had a night at the "Admiral Benbow" when I had half as much work. I was dog-tired when, a little before dawn, the crew began to raise the anchor. I might have been twice as weary, yet I would not have left the deck. All was so new and interesting to me—the brief commands, the shrill note of the whistle, the men hurrying to their places in the glow of the ship's lanterns.

"Now, Long John, sing a song," cried one voice.

"The old one," cried another.

"Ay, ay, mates," said Long John, who was standing by with his crutch under his arm, and at once broke out in the tune and words I knew so well:

"Fifteen men on the dead man's chest"—

and then the whole crew sang the chorus:

"Yo-ho-ho, and a bottle of rum!"

Even at that exciting moment it carried me back to the old "Admiral Benbow" in a second, and I seemed to hear the voice of the captain singing in the chorus. But soon the anchor was up; soon it was hanging dripping at the bows; soon the sails began to fill and the land to slip by on either side. Before I could lie down to snatch an hour of sleep the *Hispaniola* had begun her voyage to the Isle of Treasure.*

The voyage was fairly successful. The ship proved to be a good one, the crew were capable seamen, and the captain thoroughly understood his business. But before we came the length of Treasure Island, two or three things happened which I must relate.

Mr. Arrow, first of all, turned out even worse than the captain had feared. He had no command among the men, and people did what they pleased with him. But that was by no means the worst of it; for after a day or two at sea he began to appear on deck with hazy eye, red cheeks, and other signs that he had been drinking. Time after time he was ordered to go below in shame. Sometimes he fell and cut himself; sometimes he lay all day long in his cabin; sometimes for a day or two he would be almost sober and attend to his work fairly well.

In the meantime, we could never make out where he got the drink. When we asked him to his face, he would only laugh, if he were drunk. And if he were sober, he would deny that he ever tasted anything but water.

He was not only useless as an officer and a bad influence among the men, but it was plain that at this rate he would soon kill himself. So nobody was much surprised nor very sorry, when one dark night, in a heavy sea, he disappeared entirely and was seen no more.

But there we were without a mate; and it was necessary, of course, to choose another man. Job Anderson was the next best man aboard, and he was

* Isle of Treasure: another name for Treasure Island.

chosen to serve as mate. Mr. Trelawney had followed the sea, and his knowledge made him very useful, for he often took a watch himself in easy weather. Israel Hands, too, was a cunning, experienced old seaman, who could be trusted in a pinch with almost anything.

He was a great comrade of Long John Silver, and so the mention of his name leads me on to speak of our ships' cook.

Aboard ship he carried his crutch by a cord around his neck, to have both hands as free as possible. It was something to see him push the foot of the crutch against the wall and, propped against it, swaying with every movement of the ship, get on with his cooking like someone safe ashore. Still more strange was it to see him cross the deck in the heaviest of weather. He had a rope or two put up to help him across the widest spaces. He would hand himself from one place to another, now using the crutch, now trailing it alongside by the cord, as quickly as another man could walk. Yet some of the men who had sailed with him before felt sorry to see him so crippled.

"He's no common man," said Israel Hands to me. "He went to school in his young days and can speak like a book when he wishes; and brave—a lion's nothing alongside of Long John! I seen him seize four men and knock their heads together."

All the crew respected and even obeyed him. He had a way of talking to each, and doing everybody some little service. To me he was kind, and was always glad to see me in the galley, which he kept as clean as a new pin, the dishes all shining, and his parrot in a cage in one corner.

"Come away, Hawkins," he would say, "come and have a talk with John. Nobody more welcome than

yourself, my son. Sit you down and hear the news.
Here's Cap'n Flint—I calls my parrot Cap'n Flint after
the famous pirate—here's Flint wishing success to our
voyage. Wasn't you, cap'n?

And the parrot would say very rapidly, "Pieces of
eight!* Pieces of eight! Pieces of eight!" till you wondered that it was not out of breath, or till John threw
his handkerchief over the cage.

"Now, that bird," he would say, "is, maybe, 200
years old, Hawkins—they lives forever mostly; and if
anybody's seen more wickedness, it must be the devil
himself. She's sailed with England, the great Cap'n
England, the pirate. She was there when they raised
the wrecked ships that carried so much money. That's
where she learned 'Pieces of eight,' and no wonder—
there were 350,000 pieces of eight on that ship, Jim.
She's been all over the world; and to look at her you
would think she was a baby. But you smelt powder—
didn't you, cap'n—I mean, she has seen battles."

"Stand by to go about," the parrot would scream.

"Ah, she's a handsome bird, she is," the cook
would say, and give her sugar from his pocket, and
then the bird would peck at the bars and swear straight
on, wickedly. "There," John would add, "you can't
touch dirt and not be soiled, lad. Here's this poor old
innocent bird of mine swearing blue fire and none the
wiser, you may lay to that. She would swear the same
before the preacher." And John would touch his forehead with a sober way he had that made me think he
was the best of men.

---

* Pieces of Eight: Spanish silver dollars.

In the meantime, squire and Captain Smollett were still not friendly with one another. The squire made no bones about the matter. He despised the captain. The captain, on his part, never spoke but when he was spoken to, and then sharp and short and dry, and not a word wasted. He said that he must have been wrong about the crew, that some of them were as active as he wanted to see, and all had behaved fairly well. As for the ship, he had taken a great fancy to her. "But," he would add, "all I say is we're not home again, and I don't like the cruise."

At this, the squire would turn away and march up and down the deck, chin in air.

"A little more of that man," he would say, "and I shall explode."

We had some heavy weather, which only proved the worth of the *Hispaniola*. Every man on board seemed well content, and they must have been hard to please if they had been otherwise; for it is my belief there was never a ship's company so spoiled since Noah* put to sea. Double portions of rum were given on the least excuse. If the squire heard it was any man's birthday, there was plum pudding** for everyone. And always a barrel of apples stood open, for anyone to help himself if he wished.

"Never knew good come of it yet," the captain said to Dr. Livesey. "Spoil the ship's hands, make devils. That's my belief."

But good did come of the apple barrel, as you shall

---

*Noah: Biblical figure who built a vessel in which he, his family, and animals survived the Flood.

**Plum Pudding: a rich steamed or boiled pudding containing raisins, currants, citron, spices, etc.

hear. For if it had not been for that, we should have had no warning, and might all have perished.

This was how it came about.

It was about the last day of our outward voyage. Some time that night, or, at latest, before noon of the next day, we should sight Treasure Island. We were heading S.S.W., and had a steady breeze and a quiet sea. All sails, upper and lower, were full. Everyone was in the best of spirits, because we were now so near an end of the first part of our adventure.

Now, just after sunset, when all my work was over, and I was on my way to my cabin, I thought that I should like an apple. I ran on deck. The watch was all forward looking out for the island. The man steering was watching the sail and whistling away gently to himself; and that was the only sound excepting the wash of the sea against the bows and around the sides of the ship.

I climbed into the apple barrel and found there was scarcely an apple left. But, sitting down there in the dark, what with the sound of the waters and the rocking movement of the ship, I had either fallen asleep, or was on the point of doing so, when a heavy man sat down close by. The barrel shook as he leaned his shoulders against it, and I was just about to jump up when the man began to speak. It was Silver's voice and, before I had heard a dozen words, I would not have shown myself for all the world, but lay there, trembling and listening in extreme fear and curiosity. For from these dozen words I understood that the lives of all the honest men aboard depended upon me alone.

11 What I Heard in the Apple Barrel

"No, not I," said Silver. "Flint was cap'n; I had charge of steering and other easy work because of my wooden leg. The same battle I lost my leg, old Pew lost his eyes. It was a good doctor, him that cut off my leg—a college man—and what not; but he was hanged like a dog like the rest of the pirates. That bad luck came from changing the name of the ship. Now, what a ship was named, so let her stay, I says. That's the way it was with the old *Walrus,* Cap'n Flint's old ship, as I've seen running red with blood and fit to sink with gold."

"Ah," cried another voice, that of the youngest hand on board, and evidently full of admiration, "he was the flower of the flock, was Flint!"

"First I sailed with Cap'n England," said Silver, "and then with Cap'n Flint, that's my story; and now here on the *Hispaniola.* I saved 900 pounds* safe, from the trip with Cap'n England, and 2,000 after Flint. That ain't bad for a man before the mast**—all safe in the bank. 'Tain't earning now, it's saving that makes you rich, and you may lay to that. Where's all Cap'n England's men now? I dunno. Where's Flint's? Why, most of them are aboard here on the *Hispaniola,* and glad to get the plum pudding. Some of them been so

---

*Pound: a British unit of money equal to about 4.86 U.S. dollars when this story was written.

** Mast: a pole to which the sails are fastened, set upright on a ship. The *Mainmast* is the largest, and is in the center of the ship; the *Mizzenmast* is nearest the stern, or rear.

poor they been begging before that. Old Pew, as had lost his sight, spent his 1,200 pounds in a year. Where is he now? Well, he's dead now and buried. But for two years before that, shiver my timbers, the man was starving! He begged, and he stole, and he cut throats, and starved at that, by the powers! All because he didn't save his money."

"Well, it ain't much use, after all," said the young seaman.

" 'Tain't much use for fools, you may lay to it— that, nor nothing," cried Silver. "But now, look here. You're young, you are, but you're as smart as paint. I see that when I set my eyes on you, and I'll talk to you like a man."

You may imagine how I felt when I heard this disgusting old rascal speaking to another in the very same flattering tones that he had used to myself. I think, if I had been able, that I would have killed him through the barrel. Meantime, he ran on, little thinking that I was listening.

"Here it is about gentlemen of fortune. They live rough and they risk hanging, but they eat and drink well, and when a cruise is done, why, they have hundreds of pounds instead of hundreds of pennies in their pockets. Now, the most of them spends their money for rum and a good time, and then back to sea again, with nothing left but their shirts after all their money is gone. But that's not the way I do it. I puts it all away, some here, some there, and none too much anywhere so that no one will know how much I have, and wonder how I got it. I'm 50, mind you. Once back from this cruise, I will be a real gentleman in earnest. Time enough, too, says you. Ah, but I've lived easy in the meantime; never denied myself of nothing, and slept soft and ate well all my days, except when at sea. And how did I begin? Before the mast, a common seaman, like you!"

"Well," said the other, "but all your money's gone now, ain't it? You dare not show your face in Bristol after this."

"Why, where might you suppose it was?" asked Silver.

"At Bristol, in banks and places," answered his companion.

"It were," said the cook. "It were when we set sail. But my old missis has it all by now. And the 'Spyglass' is sold and the old girl's off to meet me. I would tell you where, for I trust you; but it would make jealousy among the mates."

"And can you trust your missis?" asked the other.

"Gentlemen of fortune," returned the cook, "usually trusts little among themselves, and right they are, you may lay to it. But I have a way with me, I have. When a mate tries to fool me, he won't be in the same world with old John Silver for long. There was some that was feared of Pew, and some that was feared of Flint; but Flint his own self was feared of me. Feared he was, and proud. They was the roughest crew on the sea, was Flint's. The devil himself would have been feared to go to sea with them. Well now, I tell you, I'm not a boasting man and you seen yourself how easy I get along with the men; but when I was in Flint's crew, we were the roughest and toughest pirates of all. Ah, you may be sure of yourself in old John's ship."

"Well, I tell you now," replied the lad, "I didn't half like the idea till I had this talk with you, John; but there's my hand on it now."

"And a brave lad you were, and smart, too," answered Silver, shaking hands so heartily that all the barrel shook, "and a finer lad for a gentleman of fortune I never clapped my eyes on."

By this time I had begun to understand the meaning of their words. By a "gentleman of fortune" they plainly meant a common pirate, and the little scene that I had heard was the last act in turning an honest man into a pirate. Just as I was wondering if any man on board was still loyal, Silver gave a little whistle and a third man walked up and sat down by the party.

"Dick's with us," said Silver.

"Oh, I knowed Dick would join us," returned the voice of Israel Hands. "He's no fool, is Dick." And he turned his tobacco in his mouth. "But look here," he went on, "here's what I want to know, Long John — how long are we a-going to stand off and wait before we seize the ship? I've had almost enough of Cap'n Smollett. He's been giving me orders long enough, by thunder! I want to go into that cabin, I do. I want their pickles and wines, and all that."

"Israel," said Silver, "your head ain't much account and never was. But you're able to hear, I reckon; at least, your ears is big enough. Now, here's what I say: you'll not go near the cabin; you'll stay forward with the rest of the crew. And you'll live hard, and you'll speak soft, and you'll keep sober, till I give the word; and you may lay to that, my son."

"Well, I don't say no, do I?" growled Israel. "What I say is when? That's what I say."

"When! By the powers!" cried Silver. "Well now, if you want to know, I'll tell you when. It will be the last moment I can make it, and that's when. Cap'n Smollett's a first-rate seaman, and we need him to sail the ship for us. The squire and doctor have the map—I don't know where it is, do I? Neither do you. Well then, I mean that this squire and doctor shall find the treasure, and help us to get it aboard. Then we'll see. If I was sure of you all, I'd have Cap'n Smollett sail us half way back again before I struck."

"Why, we're all seamen here, I should think," said the lad Dick.

"We're all common seamen, you mean," snapped Silver. "We can steer a ship, but we need a captain to set the course. If I had my way, I'd have Cap'n Smollett work us half way back at least; then we'd have no mistakes and get off our course. But I know the sort you are. I'll finish them at the island as soon as the treasure's on board, to please the rest of you, and a pity it is. But you're never happy till you're drunk. Split my sides, I'm a fool to sail with the likes of you!"

"Easy all, Long John," cried Israel. "Who's a-crossing of you?"

"Why, how many lads do you think I've seen hanged?" cried Silver, "and all for this same hurry and hurry and hurry. You hear me? I seen a thing or two at sea, I have. If you would only make careful plans and go slow, you would be rich, you would. But not you! I know you. You'll have your mouthful of rum tomorrow, and go hang."

"Everybody knows you are a kind of a preacher, John; but there's others that could steer as well as you," said Israel. "They like a bit of fun, they do. They aren't as strict as you but like a good time, like jolly companions every one."

"So?" says Silver. "Well, and where are they now? Pew was that sort, and he died a beggar. Flint was, and he died of rum across the sea. Ah, they was a sweet crew, they was! Only, where are they?"

"But," asked Dick, "when we do seize the ship, what are we to do with them, anyhow?"

"There's the man for me!" cried Silver with admiration. "That's what I call business. Well, what would you think? Put them ashore somewhere? That would have been Cap'n England's way. Or cut them down like that much pork? That would have been Cap'n Flint's or Billy Bones's way."

"Billy was the man for that," said Israel. " 'Dead men don't bite,' says he. Well, he's dead now himself; but if ever there was a rough hand, it was Billy."

"Right you are," said Silver, "rough and ready. But remember this: I'm an easy man—I'm quite the gentleman—but this time it's serious. Duty is duty, mates. I give you my idea what we should do with them. It's death! When I'm back in England with my share of the treasure, I don't want none of these men in the cabin a-coming home when no one is expecting them. Wait is what I say. But when the time comes, why, then do the thing right."

"John," cries Israel, "you're a man!"

"You'll say so, Israel, when you see," said Silver. "Only one thing I claim—I claim Trelawney. I'll wring his calf's head off his body with these hands. Dick!" he added, breaking off, "you just jump up, like a sweet lad, and get me an apple."

You may fancy the terror I was in! I should have leaped out and run for it, if I had found the strength, but I could not. I heard Dick begin to rise, and then someone seemed to stop him, and the voice of Hands exclaimed:

"Oh, don't do that! Don't you go eating of an apple, John. Let's have a drink of rum."

"Dick," said Silver, "I trust you. There's the key. You fill a can and bring it up."

Frightened as I was, I could not help thinking to myself that this must have been how Mr. Arrow got the strong drink that destroyed him.

Dick was gone but a little while, and during his absence Israel spoke straight on in Silver's ear. It was but a word or two that I could catch, and yet I gathered some important news. For, besides other bits that meant the same thing, this whole sentence was clear: "Not another man of them will join." So there were still faithful men on board!

When Dick returned, one after another of the three took the can and drank—one "To luck;" another with a "Here's to old Flint;" and Silver himself saying, in a kind of song, "Here's to ourselves, and hold your luff, plenty of prizes and plenty of duff."

Just then a sort of brightness fell upon me in the barrel, and looking up, I found the moon had risen and was silvering the sails. Almost at the same time the voice of the lookout shouted, "Land ho!"

12 *Council of War*

There was a great rush of feet across the deck. I could hear people tumbling up from the cabin and from the crew's quarters in the fore* part of the ship. Slipping in an instant outside my barrel, I dived behind the foresail and came out upon the open deck in time to join Hunter and Dr. Livesey in the rush for the bow.

All hands were already there. The fog had lifted almost at the same moment the moon rose. Away to the southwest of us we saw two low hills, about a couple of miles apart, and rising behind one of them a third and higher hill, whose peak was still buried in the fog. All three seemed sharp and cone-shaped.

So much I saw almost in a dream, for I had not yet got over my horrid fear of a minute or two before. Then I heard the voice of Captain Smollett giving orders. The *Hispaniola* now sailed a course that would just clear the island on the east.

"And now, men," said the captain, "has any one of you ever seen that land ahead?"

"I have, sir," said Silver. "I've been there with a ship I was cook in."

"The harbor is on the south, behind a small island, I fancy?" asked the captain.

"Yes, sir. Skeleton Island they calls it. It were a favorite place of pirates once. That hill to the north they calls the Foremast Hill. There are three hills in a row running southward—fore, main, and mizzen, sir.

* Fore or Forward: the front part of the ship. The common sailor lives here.

But the main—that's the big one with the cloud on it—they usually calls the Spyglass.

"I have a chart here," says Captain Smollett. "See if that's the place."

Long John's eyes burned in his head as he took the chart; but, by the fresh look of the paper, I knew he would be disappointed. This was not the map we found in Billy Bones's chest, but an exact copy, complete in all things except the red crosses and the written notes. Silver had the strength of mind to hide his disappointment.

"Yes, sir," said he, "this is the spot, to be sure; and very prettily drawed out. Who might have done that, I wonder? Ay, here it is! 'Capt Kidd's Harbor' they calls it. There's a strong current runs along the south, and then away north up the west coast."

"Thank you, my man," says Captain Smollett. "I'll ask you, later on, to help us. You may go."

I was surprised at the coolness with which John spoke about the island; and I admit I was half-frightened when I saw him drawing nearer to myself. He did not know, to be sure, that I had heard his talk from the apple barrel. And yet I had by this time taken such a horror of his cruelty, cunning, and power, that I could scarcely hide a shiver when he laid his hand upon my arm.

"Ah," says he, "this here is a sweet spot, this island—a sweet spot for a lad to get ashore on. You'll bathe, and you'll climb trees, and you'll hunt goats, you will. You'll climb high on them hills like a goat yourself. Why, it makes me young again. I was going to forget my timber leg, I was. It's a pleasant thing to be young and have ten toes, and you may lay to that. When you want to do a bit of exploring, you just ask old John, and he'll put up a lunch for you to take along."

And clapping me in a friendly way upon the shoulder, he hobbled off forward and went below.

Captain Smollett, the squire, and Dr. Livesey were talking together on the deck and, anxious as I was to tell them my story, I dared not interrupt them openly. While I was still trying to find some good excuse, Dr. Livesey called me to his side. He had left his pipe below and, being a slave to tobacco, had meant that I should bring it; but as soon as I was near enough to speak and not be overheard, I broke out immediately —"Doctor, let me speak. Get the captain and squire down to the cabin, and then make some excuse to send for me. I have terrible news."

The doctor looked a little startled, but next moment he was master of himself.

"Thank you, Jim," said he, quite loudly, "that was all I wanted to know," as if he had asked me a question.

And with that he turned on his heel and joined the other two. They spoke together for a little, and though none of them looked startled, or raised his voice, or so much as whistled, it was plain enough that Dr. Livesey had told them; for the next thing that I heard was the captain giving an order to Job Anderson, and all hands were called on deck.

"My lads," said Captain Smollett, "I've a word to say to you. This land that we have sighted is the place we have been sailing for. I have just told Mr. Trelawney that every man on board had done his duty, below and above, as I never ask to see it done better. He and I and the doctor are going below to the cabin to drink to your health and luck. You'll have rum served out for you to drink to our health and luck. I'll tell you what I think of this. I think it handsome. And if you think as I do, you'll give a good cheer for the gentleman that does it."

The cheer followed—that was a matter of course. It rang out so full and hearty that I confess I could hardly believe these same men were plotting for our blood.

"One more cheer for Cap'n Smollett," cried Long John. And this also was given with a will.

After that, the three gentlemen went below, and not long after, word was sent forward that Jim Hawkins was wanted in the cabin.

I found them all three seated round the table, a bottle of Spanish wine and some fruit before them. The doctor was smoking away, with his wig on his lap. That, I knew, was a sign that he was troubled. The rear window was open, for it was a warm night, and you could see the moon shining on the sea behind the ship.

"Now, Hawkins," said the squire, "you have something to say. Speak up."

I did as I was told and, as short as I could make it, gave them the whole story of Silver's talk. Nobody interrupted me till I was done, nor did any one of the three of them make so much as a movement, but they kept their eyes upon my face from first to last.

"Jim," said Dr. Livesey, "take a seat."

And they made me sit down at the table beside them, poured me out a glass of wine, and filled my hands with fruit. All three, one after the other, and each with a bow, drank to my good health for my luck and courage.

"Now, captain," said the squire, "you were right and I was wrong. I was a fool, and I await your orders."

"No more a fool than I, sir," returned the captain. "I never heard of a crew that meant to mutiny but did not show signs before, for any man that had an eye in his head to see the mischief and take steps according. But this crew," he added, "beats me."

"Captain," said the doctor, "that's Silver. A very remarkable man."

"He'd look remarkably well hanging, sir," returned the captain. "But this is talk. This don't lead to anything. I see three or four points, and with Mr. Trelawney's permission, I'll name them."

"You, sir, are the captain. It is for you to speak," says Mr. Trelawney, grandly.

"First point," began Mr. Smollett. "We must go on, because we can't turn back. If I gave the word to turn about, they would rise at once. Second point, we have time before us—at least, until this treasure's found. Third point, there are faithful hands. Now, sir, it's got to come to blows sooner or later; and what I say is, strike the first blow some fine day when they least expect it. We can count, I take it, on your own home servants, Mr. Trelawney?"

"As upon myself," declared the squire.

"Three," said the captain, "ourselves make seven, counting Hawkins, here. Now, about the honest hands?"

"Most likely Trelawney's own men," said the doctor; "those he had picked up for himself before he lit on Silver."

"No," replied the squire. "Israel Hands was one of mine."

"I did think I could have trusted Hands," added the captain.

"And to think that they're all Englishmen!" broke out the squire. "Sir, I could find it in my heart to blow the ship up."

"Well, gentlemen," said the captain, "the best that I can say is not much. We must not make any move, if you please, but keep a bright lookout. It will be hard to do, I know. It would be more pleasant to come to blows. But there's no help for it till we know our men."

"Jim here," said the doctor, "can help us more than anyone. The men are not shy with him."

"Hawkins, I put great faith in you," added the squire.

I began to feel pretty desperate at this, for I felt altogether helpless; and yet, by an odd train of events, it was indeed through me that safety came. In the meantime, talk as we pleased, there were only seven out of the twenty-six whom we knew we could trust. Out of these seven one was a boy, so that the grown men on our side were six to their nineteen.

Book 3

My Shore Adventure

13 *How My Shore Adventure Began*

The appearance of the island when I came on deck next morning was altogether changed. Although there was now no breeze, we had made a great deal of way during the night, and were now standing out about half a mile to the southeast of the low eastern coast. Gray woods covered a large part of the surface. This even color was broken up by streaks of yellow sand in the lower lands, and by many tall pine trees, taller than the rest of the woods—some alone, some in groups. The hills ran up clear above the trees in points of bare rock. All were strangely formed. The Spyglass, which was the tallest on the island, was the strangest in shape, running up steeply from almost every side, and then suddenly cut off at the top like a table.

The *Hispaniola* was rolling in the ocean swell. The whole ship was creaking, groaning, and jumping. I had to cling tight to the rope, and the world turned around before my eyes. For though I was a good enough sailor when the ship was under way, this standing still and being rolled about like a bottle was a thing I never learned to stand, above all in the morning before breakfast.

Perhaps it was this—perhaps it was the look of the island, with its gray, lonely-looking woods, and wild stone peaks, and the waves that we could both see and hear foaming and thundering on the steep beach that disgusted me with the place. The sun shone bright and hot, and the shore birds were fishing and crying all around us, and you would have thought anyone would be glad to get to land after being so long at sea. But my heart sank into my boots, and ever after that first look, I hated the very thought of Treasure Island.

We had a hard morning's work before us, for there was no sign of any wind, and the boats had to be got out and manned, and the ship worked along three or four miles round the corner of the island and up the narrow passage to the harbor behind Skeleton Island. I got into one of the boats, where I had, of course, no business. The heat was great and the men grumbled fiercely over their work. Anderson was in command of my boat, and instead of keeping the crew in order, he grumbled as loud as the worst.

"Well," he said, with an oath, "It's not for ever."

I thought this was a very bad sign; for, up to that day, the men had gone quickly and willing about their business.

All the way in, Long John guided the ship. He knew the passage like the palm of his hand, and never hesitated once.

We anchored just where the anchor was in the chart, about a third of a mile from each shore, the mainland on one side and Skeleton Island on the other. The bottom was clean sand. The plunge of our anchor sent up clouds of birds wheeling and crying over the woods; but in less than a minute they were down again, and all was once more silent.

The land on all sides of us was covered with woods, the trees coming right down to the water's edge. The shores were mostly flat, and the hilltops stood round at a distance in a sort of half circle, one here, one there. Two little rivers, or rather, two swamps, emptied out into the harbor. From the ship we could see nothing of the fort, for it was hidden among trees. If it had not been for the chart, we might have thought ourselves the first that had ever anchored there since the island arose out of the seas.

There was not a breath of air moving, nor a sound but that of the sea booming half a mile away along the beaches and against the rocks outside. A queer foul smell hung over the harbor—a smell of water-soaked leaves and rotting tree trunks. I noticed the doctor sniffing and sniffing, like someone tasting a bad egg.

"I don't know about treasure," he said, "but I'm quite sure there's fever here."

If the actions of the men had been alarming in the boat, they became more so when the crew came aboard. They lay about the deck talking together in low tones and growling. The slightest order was received with a black look, and almost not obeyed. Mutiny, it was plain, hung over us like a thundercloud.

And it was not only we of the cabin party who saw the danger. Long John was hard at work going from group to group giving good advice, and no man could have shown a better example. He obeyed eagerly and with courtesy, and he was all smiles to everyone. If an order were given, John would be on his crutch in an instant, with the most cheerful "Ay, ay, sir!" in the world; and when there was nothing else to do, he kept up one song after another, as if to hide the discontent of the rest.

Of all the gloomy features of that gloomy afternoon, this anxiety on the part of Long John seemed to be the worst.

We gathered in the cabin to talk things over.

"Sir," said the captain, "if I risk another order the whole ship will come about our ears on the run. You see, sir, here it is. Suppose I get a rough answer. Well, if I answer back, the fight will begin at once. If I don't, Silver will see there's something queer about that, and the game's up. Now, we've only one man to depend on."

"And who is that?" asked the squire.

"Silver, sir," returned the captain. "He's as anxious as you and I to smooth things over. This is a quarrel. He'd soon talk them out of it if he had the chance, and what I think we ought to do is to give him the chance. Let's allow the men an afternoon ashore. If they all go, why, we'll hold the ship. If none of them go, well, then, we hold the cabin, and God defend the right. If some go, you mark my words, sir, Silver will bring them aboard again as mild as lambs."

It was so decided. Loaded pistols were served out to all the sure men. Hunter, Joyce, and Redruth were told the whole story, and received the news with less surprise and a better spirit than we had looked for. The captain then went on deck and talked to the crew.

"My lads," said he, "we've had a hot day and are all tired and out of sorts. A trip ashore will hurt nobody —the boats are still in the water. You can take the gigs,* and as many as please may go ashore for the afternoon. I'll fire a gun half an hour before sundown."

I believe the silly fellows must have thought they would find the treasure as soon as they were landed. They all came out of their gloom in a moment, and gave a cheer that started the echo in a far-away hill and sent the birds once more flying and screaming round the harbor.

*Gig: a small boat belonging to a ship and rowed with oars, used for carrying men and officers.

The captain was too bright to be in the way. He whipped out of sight in a moment, leaving Silver to arrange the party.

At last the party was made up. Six fellows were to stay on board, and the remaining thirteen, including Silver, began to get into the gigs.

Then it was that there came into my head the first of the mad notions that did so much to save our lives. If six men were left by Silver, it was plain our party could not take and fight the ship; and since only six were left it was equally plain that the cabin party had no present need of my help. I decided at once to go ashore. In a second I had slipped over the side and curled up in the fore of the nearest boat, and almost at the same moment she pushed off.

No one took notice of me, only the front man saying, "Is that you, Jim? Keep your head down." But Silver, from the other boat, looked sharply over and called out to know if that were me. From that moment I began to regret what I had done.

The crews raced for the beach. But the boat I was in, having a good start, and being at once the lighter and rowed by the best men, shot far ahead of the other, and the bow soon struck the shore among the trees. I caught a branch and swung myself out and plunged into the nearest bushes, while Silver and the rest were still a hundred yards behind.

"Jim, Jim!" I heard him shouting.

But you may be sure I paid no heed. Jumping, ducking and breaking through, I ran straight before my nose till I could run no longer.

14 *The First Blow*

I was so pleased at having given the slip to Long John that I began to enjoy myself and look around me with some interest on the strange land that I was in.

I had crossed a marshy spot full of willows and odd, swampy trees. I now came out upon the edge of an open piece of rolling, sandy country about a mile long, dotted with a few pines and a great number of twisted trees, like the oak in growth, but with pale leaves like willows. On the far side of the open space stood one of the hills, with two peaks shining brightly in the sun.

I now felt for the first time the joy of exploring. No people lived on the island. I had left my shipmates behind, and nothing lived in front of me but animals and birds. I ran about among the trees. Here and there were flowering plants, strange to me. Here and there I saw snakes, and one raised his head from a rock and made a noise like the spinning of a top. Little did I dream that he was a deadly enemy, and that the noise was the famous rattle.

Then I came to a thick growth of these odd trees which grew low along the sand like bushes. The woods stretched down from the top of one of the sandy hills, spreading and growing taller as it went. Where it reached the edge of the swamp, a little river made its way into the harbor.

All at once there began to be a sort of rustle among the reeds. A wild duck flew up with a cry, another followed, and soon over the whole surface of the marsh a great cloud of birds hung screaming and circling in the air. I knew at once that some of my shipmates must be drawing near along the edge of the swamp. Nor was I wrong. For soon I heard the very distant and low tones of a human voice, which, as I listened, grew steadily louder and nearer.

This put me in a great fear, and I crawled under cover of the nearest oak and hid there, as quiet as a mouse.

Another voice answered; and then the first voice, which I now knew to be Silver's, once more took up the story and ran on for a long while, only now and again interrupted by the other. By the sound they must have been talking earnestly and almost fiercely. But no single word came to my hearing.

At last the speakers paused, and perhaps sat down. For they did not come any nearer, and the birds themselves began to grow more quiet, and to settle again to their places in the swamp.

Now I began to feel that I was not doing my business. That since I had been so foolish as to come ashore with these rascals, the least I could do was to listen to what they were saying. My plain duty was to draw as close as I could, under cover of the low trees.

I could tell the direction of the speakers pretty exactly, not only by the sound of their voices, but by the actions of the few birds that still hung in alarm above their heads.

Crawling on all fours, I made steadily but slowly toward them. At last, raising my head to an open space among the leaves, I could see clear down into a little green valley beside the marsh, where Long John Silver and another of the crew stood face to face talking.

The sun beat full upon them. Silver had thrown his hat beside him on the ground, and his great, smooth, blond face, all shining with heat, was lifted to the other man's as though asking something of him.

"Mate," he was saying, "it's because I thinks well of you! If I hadn't, do you think I'd be here warning you? The plans are made—you can't change them. It's to save your neck that I'm speaking, and if one of the others knew it, where would I be, Tom—now tell me, where would I be?"

"Silver," said the other man—and I saw that he was red in the face, and his voice shook, too, like a tight rope—"Silver," says he, "you're old; and you're honest, or are supposed to be; and you've money, too; and you're brave. And will you tell me you'll let yourself be led away with these rascals? As sure as God sees me, I'd sooner lose my hand. If I turn against my duty——"

And then all of a sudden he was interrupted by a noise. I had found one of the honest hands—well, here, at that same moment, came news of another. Far away out in the marsh there arose, all of a sudden, a sound like the cry of anger, then another right after it; and then one horrid, long-drawn scream. The rocks of the Spyglass echoed it again and again. The whole flock of birds rose again. Long after that death yell was still ringing in my brain, silence had fallen, and only the rustle of the birds and the roar of the distant waves could be heard in the quiet of the afternoon.

Tom had leaped at the sound but Silver had not winked an eye. He stood where he was, resting lightly on his crutch, watching his companion like a snake about to spring.

"John!" said the sailor, stretching out his hand.

"Hands off!" cried Silver, leaping back a yard, as it seemed to me.

"Hands off, if you like, John Silver," said the other. "It's a black conscience that can make you feared of me. But, in heaven's name, tell me what was that?"

"That?" returned Silver, smiling away, but more watchful than ever, his eye a mere pinpoint in his big face, but gleaming like a bit of glass. "That? Oh, I reckon that'll be Alan."

And at this poor Tom spoke out like a hero.

"Alan!" he cried. "Then rest his soul for a true seaman! And as for you, John Silver, long you've been a mate of mine, but you're mate of mine no more. If I die like a dog, I'll die in my duty. You've killed Alan, have you? Kill me, too, if you can. But I will not join you."

And with that, this brave fellow turned his back directly on the cook, and set off walking for the beach. But he was not to go far. With a cry, John seized the branch of a tree, whipped the crutch from under his arm, and sent it flying through the air. It struck poor Tom, point first and with great force, right between the shoulders in the middle of his back. His hands flew up, he gave a sort of gasp, and fell.

Whether he were hurt much or little, none could ever tell. Likely enough, to judge from the sound, his back was broken on the spot. But he had no time given him to recover. Silver, quick as a flash, even without leg or crutch, was on the top of him next moment, and had twice buried his knife deep into Tom's body. From my place of hiding, I could hear him pant aloud as he struck the blows.

I do not know what it is to faint, but I do know that for the next little while the whole world swam away from before me in a whirling mist. Silver and the birds, and the tall Spyglass hilltop went round and round before my eyes, and all kinds of bells rang and distant voices shouted in my ears.

When I came again to myself, the monster had pulled himself together, his crutch under his arm, his hat upon his head. Just before him, Tom lay motionless upon the grass. The man who murdered him paid no attention to him, but began to clean his blood-stained knife calmly upon the grass. Everything else was the same, the sun still shone brightly on the marsh and the tall peak of the mountain. I could scarcely believe that murder had really been done, and a human life cruelly cut short a moment ago before my eyes.

But now John put his hand into his pocket, brought out a whistle, and blew upon it several low blasts that rang far across the heated air. I could not tell, of course, the meaning of the signal; but it instantly awoke my fears. More men would be coming. I might be discovered. They had already slain two of the honest people. After Tom and Alan, might not I come next?

Instantly I began to crawl back again, with what speed and silence I could manage, to the more open part of the woods. As I did so, I could hear shouts coming and going between the old pirate and his comrades, and this sound of danger lent me wings. As soon as I was clear of the bushes, I ran as I never ran before, not caring what direction so long as it led me from the seamen. And as I ran, fear grew and grew upon me.

Indeed, could anyone be more entirely lost than I? When the gun fired, how should I dare to go down to the boats among those terrible men, still smoking from their crime? Would not the first of them who saw me kill me at once? If I stayed behind, would it not be a proof to them of my fears? It was all over, I thought. Good-bye to the *Hispaniola;* good-bye to the squire, the doctor, and the captain! There was nothing left for me but to starve to death, or to die by the hands of the mutineers.

All this while, as I say, I was still running. I had drawn near to the foot of the little hill with the two peaks, and had got into a part of the island where the small oak trees grew more widely apart, and seemed more like forest trees in size and shape. Mixed with these were a few scattered pines, some 50, some nearer 70 feet high. The air, too, smelled more pure than down beside the marsh.

And here a fresh alarm brought me to stop with a fiercely pounding heart.

15 *The Man of the Island*

From the side of the hill, which was steep and stony, a bit of gravel fell rattling and bounding through the trees. I looked in that direction, and saw a figure leap with great speed behind the trunk of a pine. What it was, whether bear or man or monkey, I could not tell. But the terror of this new sight brought me to a full stop.

I was now, it seemed, cut off on both sides; behind me the mutineers,* before me this unknown thing. And immediately I began to prefer the dangers that I knew to those that I did not know. Silver himself seemed less terrible than this creature of the woods. I turned on my heel, and looking sharply behind me over my shoulder, began to return in the direction of the boats.

Instantly the figure came out from behind the pine tree and, making a wide circle, began to head me off. I could see it was in vain for me to try to outrun this creature. From trunk to trunk it raced like a deer, running manlike on two legs, but unlike any man that I had ever seen, stooping almost double as it ran. Yet a man it was, I could no longer be in doubt about that.

I began to recall what I had heard of savages. I was just about to call for help. But the mere fact that he was a man, however wild, had somewhat calmed me, and my fear of Silver began to return again. I stood still, therefore, and looked about for some way to escape. As I was so doing, the thought of my pistol

* Mutineer: a man who takes part in a mutiny.

flashed into my mind. As soon as I remembered that I had a weapon, courage glowed again in my heart. And I faced this man of the island and walked quickly toward him.

He was hidden, by this time, behind another tree trunk. But he must have been watching me closely, for as soon as I began to move in his direction he stepped out and came forward to meet me. Then he paused, drew back, came forward again, and at last, to my wonder and surprise, threw himself on his knees and held out his clasped hands to me.

At that I once more stopped.

"Who are you?" I asked.

"Ben Gunn," he answered, and his voice sounded coarse and awkward, as though he had not used it for a long time. "I'm poor Ben Gunn, I am. I haven't spoke with a Christian these three years."

I could now see that he was a man like myself, and that his face was even pleasing. His skin, wherever it showed, was burnt by the sun. Even his lips were black, and his fair eyes looked strange in so dark a face. Of all the beggars that I had seen or dreamed of, he was the most ragged. He was dressed with pieces of old ship's sails and old sea cloth, held together by brass buttons, bits of stick, and pieces of string.

"Three years!" I cried. "Were you shipwrecked?"

"Nay, mate," said he—"marooned."

I had heard the word, and I knew it stood for a horrible kind of punishment common enough among pirates. When they wished to punish a man they would "maroon" him—that is, they would put him ashore with a little powder and shot, and leave him behind on some lonely and distant island.

"Marooned three years ago," he continued, "and lived on goats since then, and berries, and fish. Wherever a man is, says I, a man can do for himself. But, mate, I'm hungry for Christian food. You haven't got a piece of cheese about you, now? No? Well, many's the long night I've dreamed of cheese—and woke up again, and here I were."

"If ever I can get aboard again," said I, "you shall have all the cheese you want."

All this time he had been feeling my coat, smoothing my hands, looking at my boots, and showing much pleasure in the presence of a fellow creature. But at my last words he looked at me sharply.

"If ever you can get aboard again, says you?" he repeated. "Why now, who's to stop you?"

"Not you, I know," was my reply.

"And right you are," he cried. "Now you—what do you call yourself, mate?"

"Jim," I told him.

"Jim, Jim," says he, quite pleased. "Well now, Jim, I've lived so rough that you'd be ashamed to hear of it. Now, you wouldn't think I had a religious mother—to look at me?" he asked.

"Why, no, not in particular," I answered.

"Ah, well," said he, "but I had—remarkable religious. And I was a polite, good boy, and could rattle off my prayers so fast that you couldn't tell one word from another. And here's what I come to, Jim, and it all begun with matching pennies with the other boys. That's what it begun with, but it went further than that. Mother told me just how it would be, she did, the good woman! But it were the good Lord that put me here. I've thought it all out in this here lonely island,

and I've made up my mind to be good again. You won't catch me tasting rum so much; but just a little bit for luck, the first chance I have. I've made up my mind to be good. And, Jim,"—looking all round him, and speaking in a whisper—"I'm rich."

I now felt sure that the poor lonely fellow had gone crazy, and I suppose I must have shown the feeling in my face; for he said again hotly:

"Rich! Rich! I says. And I'll tell you what! I'll make a rich man of you, Jim. Ah, Jim, you'll bless your stars that you was the first that found me!"

And at this there came suddenly a shadow over his face, and he held my hand tightly, and shook his finger before my eyes.

"Now, Jim, you tell me true—that ain't Flint's ship?" he asked.

At this I had a happy idea. I began to believe that I had found a friend, and I answered him at once.

"It's not Flint's ship, and Flint is dead. But I'll tell you true, as you ask me—there are some of Flint's hands aboard; worse luck for the rest of us."

"Not a man—with one—leg?" he gasped.

"Silver?" I asked.

"Ah, Silver!" says he. "That were his name."

"He's the cook, and the leader, too."

He was still holding me by the arm, and at that he gave it quite a twist.

"If you was sent by Long John," he said, "I'm as good as dead, and I know it."

I had made my mind up in a moment, and told him the whole story of our voyage, and the trouble in which we found ourselves. He heard me with the keenest interest, and when I had finished he patted me on the head.

"You're a good lad, Jim," he said, "and you're all in a tight spot, ain't you? Well, you just put your trust in Ben Gunn—Ben Gunn's the man to do it. Would you think it likely, now, that your squire would be a generous man in case I help him out of his trouble?"

I told him the squire was the most generous of men.

"Ay, but you see," returned Ben Gunn, "I didn't mean giving me a job as a gatekeeper, and such; that's not what I want, Jim. What I mean is, would he be likely to come down to the tune of, say 1,000 pounds out of money that's as good as my own already?"

"I am sure he would," said I. "As it was, all hands were to share."

"*And* a passage home?" he added, with a look of great cunning.

"Why," I cried, "the squire's a gentleman. And besides, if we got rid of the others, we should want you to help work the vessel home."

"Ah," said he, "so you would." And he seemed very much pleased.

"Now, I'll tell you what," he went on. "So much I'll tell you and no more. I were in Flint's ship when he buried the treasure, he and six others—six strong seamen. They was ashore nearly a week, and us waiting in the old *Walrus*. One fine day up went the signal, and here come Flint by himself in a little boat, and his head done up in a blue scarf. The sun was getting up, and terribly white he looked about the face. But there he was, you mind, and the six that had gone ashore with him all dead—dead and buried. How he done it, not a man among us could make out. It was battle, murder, and sudden death—him against six. Billy

Bones was the mate; Long John Silver, he was in the crew; and they asked Flint where the treasure was. 'Ah,' says he, 'you can go ashore, if you like and stay,' he says, 'but as for the ship, she'll sail away for more gold, by thunder!' That's what he said.

"Well, I was in another ship three years ago, and we sighted this island. 'Boys,' said I, 'here's Flint's treasure; let's land and find it.' The captain was angry at that, but my mates were all of a mind and landed. Twelve days they looked for it, and every day they were angrier with me, until one fine morning all hands went aboard. 'As for you, Benjamin Gunn,' says they, 'here's a gun,' they says, 'and a spade, and a pick. You can stay here, and find Flint's money for yourself,' they says.

"Well, Jim, three years have I been here, and not a bite of Christian food from that day to this."

And with that he winked and pinched me hard.

"Just you say these words to your squire, Jim," he went on. "Say this: Three years he lived on this island, light and dark, fair and rain; and sometimes he would think upon a prayer (you'll say), and sometimes he would think of his old mother, if she's alive (you'll say). But the most part of Gunn's time (this is what you'll say)—the most part of his time was took up with another matter. And then you'll give him a pinch, like I do."

And he pinched me again in the most friendly manner.

"Then," he continued, "you'll say this: Gunn is a good man (you'll say), and he puts a good deal more trust in a gentleman born than in these gentlemen of fortune, I mean pirates, having been one hisself."

"Well," I said, "I don't understand one word that

you've been saying. But that's no matter, for how am I to get on board?"

"Ah," said he, "that's the problem, for sure. Well, there's my boat that I made with my two hands. I keep her under the white rock. If the worst comes to the worst, we might try that after dark. Hi!" he broke out, "what's that?"

For just then, although the sun had still an hour or two to run, all the echoes of the island awoke and roared to the thunder of a cannon.

"They have begun to fight!" I cried. "Follow me."

And I began to run toward the harbor, my terrors all forgotten. Close at my side, the marooned man ran easily and lightly.

"Left, left," says he; "keep to your left hand, mate Jim! Under the trees with you! There's where I killed my first goat. They don't come down here now. They're all up on them mountains for fear of Benjamin Gunn."

So he kept talking as I ran, neither expecting nor receiving any answer.

The cannon shot was followed, after some time by many shots from guns and pistols.

Another pause, and then, not a quarter of a mile in front of me, I saw the Union Jack flutter in the air above a wood.

Book 4

The Fort

16 The Doctor's Story: How We Left the Ship

It was about half past one—three bells as the seamen say—when the two gigs went ashore from the *Hispaniola*. The captain, the squire, and I were talking matters over in the cabin. If there had been a breath of wind we should have fallen on the six mutineers who were left aboard with us and slipped away to sea. But there was no wind. And, to make it worse, down came Hunter with the news that Jim Hawkins had slipped into a boat and had gone ashore with the rest.

Of course we did not doubt Jim Hawkins, but we were alarmed for his safety. With the men in the temper they were in, it seemed an even chance if we should see the lad again. We ran on deck. It was an exceedingly hot day. The smell of the place turned me sick. If ever a man smelt fever it was in that harbor. The six rascals were sitting grumbling under a sail in the forward part of the ship. Ashore we could see the gigs fastened, and a man sitting in each, near the place where the river runs in. One of them was whistling "Lillibullero."

Waiting was a strain, and it was decided that Hunter and I should go ashore with another small boat, the jolly-boat,* to see what could be learned.

The gigs had gone somewhat to their right; but Hunter and I pulled straight in, in the direction of the

_____
* Jolly-boat: a small boat belonging to a ship, used to carry small loads.

fort shown upon the chart. The two who were left guarding their boats seemed excited when they saw us. "Lillibullero" stopped short, and I could see the pair talking over what they ought to do. If they had gone and told Silver, all might have been different. But they had their orders, I suppose, and sat quietly where they were and began again to whistle "Lillibullero."

There was a slight bend in the coast, and I steered so as to put it between us; and so, even before we landed we had lost sight of the gigs. I jumped out and came as near running as I dared, with a big silk handkerchief under my hat to keep me cool, a pair of pistols ready for use.

I had not gone a hundred yards when I reached the fort.

This was how it was: a spring of clear water rose almost at the top of a small hill. Well, on the hill and around the spring, they had built a stout log house, fit to hold 40 people in a pinch, with openings for guns on every side. All round this they had cleared a wide space. At the edge of the cleared space, they had built a fence six feet high, without door or opening, too strong to pull down without time and labor, and too open to shelter any who might attack. The people in the log house, then, could stand quietly in shelter and shoot the attackers like birds. All they needed was a good guard and food.

What pleased me most was the spring. For, though we had a good enough place of it in the cabin of the *Hispaniola,* with plenty of arms and powder and food, there had been one thing missing—we had no water. I was thinking this over when there came ringing over the island the cry of a man at the point of death. I was not new to violent death, having served in the army, but this cry filled me with fear. "Jim Hawkins is gone," was my first thought.

There is no time to waste in either a doctor's or a soldier's work. I made up my mind instantly, and with no time lost, returned to the shore and jumped on board the jolly-boat.

By good fortune Hunter pulled a good oar. We made the water fly; and the boat was soon alongside the *Hispaniola,* and I aboard her.

I found them all shaken, as was natural. The squire was sitting down, as white as a sheet, thinking of the harm he had led us to, the good man! Abraham Gray, one of the seamen, was little better.

"That man," said the captain, nodding toward him, "is new to this work. He nearly fainted when he heard the cry. We might get him to join us."

I told my scheme to the captain, and between us we settled on the plans for carrying it out.

"We put old Redruth to guard the gallery* between the cabin and the crew's quarters forward, with three or four loaded guns. Hunter brought the boat round under the stern of the ship, and Joyce and I set to work loading her with powder, guns, bags of bread, barrels of pork, a small barrel of rum, and my medicine chest.

In the meantime, the squire and Captain Smollett stayed on deck. The captain hailed Israel Hands, who was the most important man on board.

"Mr. Hands," he said, "here are two of us with a pair of pistols each. If any one of you six makes a sign of any kind, that man's dead."

They were greatly surprised. After talking with one another, one and all tumbled down the stairs, thinking to surprise us from the rear. But when they

---

* Gallery: a balcony or structure on the stern or forward of a vessel.

saw Redruth waiting for them in the gallery, they turned about at once, and a head popped out again on deck.

"Down, dog!" cries the captain.

And the head popped back again; and we heard no more, for the time, of these six seamen.

By this time, tumbling things in as they came, we had the jolly-boat loaded as much as we dared. Joyce and I got out at the stern, and we made for shore again as fast as oars could take us.

This second trip alarmed the watchers along the shore. "Lillibullero" was dropped again; and just before we lost sight of them behind the little point, one of them whipped ashore and disappeared. I had half a mind to change my plan and destroy their boats, but I feared that Silver and the others might be close at hand, and all might very well be lost by trying for too much.

We had soon touched land in the same place as before, and began to stock the blockhouse.* All three made the first journey, heavily loaded, and tossed our stores over the fence. Then, leaving Joyce to guard them—one man, to be sure, but with half a dozen guns—Hunter and I returned to the jolly-boat and loaded ourselves once more. So we continued without pausing to take breath, till the whole load was inside the fence. Then Joyce and Hunter took up their guard in the blockhouse, and I, with all my power, rowed back to the *Hispaniola.*

That we should have risked a second boatload seems more daring than it really was. The mutineers were greater in number than we were, of course, but not one of them had a gun. And though all carried

---

* Blockhouse: a fort made of logs, with openings for guns.

pistols, we would be able to give a good account of at least a half dozen of them before they could get close enough to use their pistols.

The squire was waiting for me at the stern window, all his faintness gone from him. He caught the rope and fastened it, and we began loading the boat for our very lives. We loaded pork, powder, and bread, with only a gun and a cutlass apiece for the squire and me and Redruth and the captain. The rest of the arms and powder we dropped over into 15 feet of water. We could see the bright steel shining far below us in the sun, on the clean, sandy bottom.

By this time the tide was beginning to go out and the ship was swinging round to her anchor. Voices were heard faintly in the direction of the two gigs. This warned our party to be off.

Redruth left his place in the gallery and dropped into the boat, which we then brought round where it would be easier for Captain Smollett to board her.

"Now, men," said he, "do you hear me?"

There was no answer from the crew's quarters.

"It's to you, Abraham Gray—it's to you I am speaking."

Still no reply.

"Gray," resumed Mr. Smollett, a little louder, "I am leaving this ship, and order you to follow your captain. I know you are a good man at heart, and I believe not one of the lot of you is as bad as he makes out. I have my watch here in my hand. I give you 30 seconds to join me."

There was a pause.

"Come, my fine fellow," continued the captain, "don't hang back so long. I'm risking my life and the lives of these good gentlemen, every second."

There was a sudden burst of noise, a sound of blows, and out rushed Abraham Gray with a knife cut on the side of the cheek. He came running to the captain, like a dog to the whistle.

"I'm with you, sir," said he.

And the next moment he and the captain had dropped into the jolly-boat, and we had pushed off and were on our way.

We were safely out of the ship, but not yet ashore in our fort.

17 The Doctor's Story Continued: The Jolly-boat's Last Trip

This fifth trip was quite different from any of the others. In the first place, the little boat that we were in had been loaded too heavily. Five grown men, and three of them—Trelawney, Redruth, and the captain—over six feet high, was already more than she was meant to carry. Add to that the powder, pork, and bread bags. The boat was low in the water, and, before we had gone a hundred yards, my clothing was soaking wet.

The captain made us balance the boat, and we got her to lie a little more evenly on the water. All the same, we were afraid to breathe.

In the second place the tide was causing a rippling current which ran out toward the sea. Even the ripples were a danger to the loaded boat. But the worst of it was that we were swept out of our course and away from the proper landing place behind the point. If we let the current have its way we should come ashore beside the gigs, where the pirates might appear at any moment.

"I cannot keep her head for the fort, sir," said I to the captain. I was steering, while he and Redruth, two fresh men, were at the oars. "The tide keeps washing her down. Could you pull a little stronger?"

"Not without sinking the boat," said he. "You must keep trying, sir, if you please—keep trying until you see you're gaining."

I tried, and found that the tide kept sweeping us westward until I had turned her head due east, or just about right angles to the way we ought to go.

"We'll never get ashore at this rate," said I.

"If it's the only course that we can lie, sir, we must even lie it," returned the captain. "We must keep upstream. You see, sir," he went on, "if we do not, it's hard to say where we should get ashore, besides the chance of being boarded by the gigs. Now, the way we are going, the current must let up, and then we can slip back along the shore."

"The current's less already, sir," said the man Gray. "You can ease her off a bit."

"Thank you, my man," said I, quite as if nothing had happened. We had all quietly made up our minds to treat him like one of ourselves.

Suddenly the captain spoke up again, and I thought his voice was a little changed.

"The gun!" said he.

"I have thought of that," said I, for I believed he was thinking that the pirates would try to land the big gun from the ship for an attack on the fort. "They could never get the gun ashore, and if they did, they could never haul it through the woods."

"Look back, doctor," replied the captain.

We had entirely forgotten the big gun; and there, to our horror, were the five rogues busy getting off its cover. Not only that, but it flashed into my mind at the same moment that the shot and the powder for the gun had been left behind, where the evil men aboard could easily get them.

"Israel was Flint's gunner," said Gray.

At any risk, we headed the boat straight for the landing place. By this time we had got so far out of the run of the current that I could keep her steady for the shore. But the worst of it was that in doing so, our boat was brought around so that our broad side was toward the *Hispaniola,* and was as easy to hit as a barn door.

I could hear, as well as see, that rum-faced rascal, Israel Hands, dropping the shot on the deck.

"Who's the best shot?" asked the captain.

"Mr. Trelawney, far and away," said I.

"Mr. Trelawney, will you please pick me off one of these men, sir? Hands, if possible," said the captain. Trelawney was as cool as steel. He examined his gun.

"Now," cried the captain, "easy with that gun, sir, or you'll sink the boat. All hands stand by to balance her when he fires."

The squire raised his gun, the rowing stopped, and we leaned over to the side to keep the balance. All was so nicely done that not a drop of water ran into the boat.

The men aboard the *Hispaniola,* by this time, had the gun pointed toward our jolly-boat, and Israel Hands, who was the gunner, was in plain view. However, we had no luck. For just as Trelawney fired, down Israel stooped, the ball whistled over him, and it was one of the other four who fell.

The cry he gave was echoed, not only by his companions on board, but by a great number of voices from the shore. Looking in that direction, I saw the other pirates running out from among the trees and tumbling into their places in the boats.

"Here come the gigs, sir," said I.

"Make haste, then," cried the captain. "We mustn't mind if we sink her now. If we can't get ashore, all's up."

Only one of the gigs is being used, sir," I added. "The crew of the other most likely is going round by shore to cut us off."

"They'll have a hot run, sir," returned the captain. "Sailors are not used to running on shore, you know. It's not them I mind. It's the shot from the big gun. We are too easy to hit. Tell us, squire, when you see them fire, and we'll hold back the boat."

In the meanwhile we had been going ahead at a good pace and very little water had run into the boat. We were now close to shore; 30 or 40 strokes and we should reach it. The gig was no longer to be feared. The little point of land had already hidden it from our eyes. The tide, which had so cruelly slowed us, was now slowing the mutineers. The one danger was the gun.

"If I dared," said the captain, "I'd stop and pick off another man."

But it was plain that they meant nothing should delay their shot. They had never so much as looked at their fallen comrade, though he was not dead, and I could see him trying to crawl away.

"Ready!" cried the squire.

"Hold!" cried the captain, quick as an echo.

And he and Redruth backed with a great push that sent the rear end of the jolly-boat under water. The report of the gun fell at the same time. This was the first shot that Jim heard, the sound of the squire's shot not having reached him. Where the ball fell, not one of us knew; but I fancy it must have been over our heads.

At any rate, the boat sank by the stern, quite gently, in three feet of water, leaving the captain and myself facing each other on our feet. The other three went completely under and came up again, wet and bubbling.

So far there was no great harm done. No lives were lost, and we could wade ashore in safety. But there were all our stores at the bottom, and, to make things worse, only two guns out of five were still dry and ready to use. I had snatched mine from my knees and held it over my head as the boat sank. As for the captain, he had carried his over his shoulder, and it did not get wet. The other three guns had gone down with the boat.

To add to our fear, we heard voices already drawing near us in the woods along shore. There was great danger that we might be cut off from the fort. Besides, we were afraid that if Hunter and Joyce were attacked by a half a dozen, they might not have the sense to stand firm. Hunter was steady, that we knew; Joyce was a doubtful case—a pleasant, polite man, but not quite fitted for a man of war.

With all this in our minds, we waded ashore as fast as we could, leaving behind us the poor jolly-boat and a good half of all our powder and stores.

18 The Doctor's Story Continued: End of the First Day's Fighting

We made our best speed across the strip of woods that divided us from the fort, and at every step we took, the voices of the pirates rang nearer. Soon we could hear them as they ran, and the cracking of the branches in the woods.

I began to see we should have trouble in earnest, and looked to my gun.

"Captain," said I, "Trelawney is the dead shot. Give him your gun. His own is useless."

They exchanged guns, and Trelawney, silent and cool as he had been since the beginning, hung a moment on his heel to see that all was ready. At the same time, seeing that Gray was not armed, I handed him my cutlass. It did all our hearts good to see him spit in his hand, frown, and make the blade sing through the air. It was plain from every line of his body that our new hand was worth his salt.

Forty paces farther we came to the edge of the wood and saw the fort in front of us. We struck the fence about the middle of the south side. Almost at the same time seven mutineers—Job Anderson at their head—came running to the southwest corner.

They paused, as if surprised. Before they had time to think, not only the squire and I, but Hunter and Joyce from the blockhouse, had time to fire. The four shots came one after another, but they did the business. One of the enemy fell, and the rest turned and plunged into the trees.

After loading our guns again, we walked down the outside of the fence to see the fallen enemy. He was stone dead—shot through the heart.

We began to rejoice over our good success, when just at that moment a pistol cracked in the bush. A ball whistled close past my ear, and poor Tom Redruth stumbled and fell his length on the ground. Both the squire and I returned the shot; but as we had nothing to aim at, it is likely we only wasted powder. Then we loaded our guns, and turned our attention to poor Tom.

The captain and Gray were already examining him, and I saw with half an eye that all was over.

I believe the speed of our return shots had scattered the mutineers once more. They did not disturb us while we got poor old Redruth lifted over the fence and carried, groaning and bleeding, into the log house.

Poor old fellow, he had not spoken one word of surprise, complaint, or fear from the very beginning of our troubles till now, when we laid him down in the log house to die. He had kept guard like a hero in the gallery; he had followed every order silently and well; he was the oldest of our party by 20 years; and now, good old servant, it was he that was to die.

The squire dropped down beside him on his knees and kissed his hand, crying like a child.

"Be I going, doctor?" he asked.

"Tom, my man," said I, "you're going home."

"I wish I had had a chance at them with the gun first," he replied.

"Tom," said the squire, "say you forgive me, won't you?"

"Would that be quite right from me to you squire?" was the answer. "However, so be it, amen!"

After a little while of silence, he said he thought somebody might read a prayer. "It's the custom, sir," he added. And not long after, without another word, he passed away.

In the meantime the captain, who seemed to be wonderfully big about the chest and pockets, had turned out a great many stores—the British colors, a Bible, a piece of thick rope, pen, ink, the log, and pounds of tobacco. He had found a long pine tree inside the fence and, with the help of Hunter, he had set it up at the corner of the log house. Then, climbing on the roof, he had with his own hand run up the colors.

This seemed to make him feel better. He went into the log house, and set about counting up the stores, as if nothing else had happened. But he had an eye on Tom for all that; and as soon as all was over, brought another flag and spread it on the body.

"Don't you take on, sir," he said, shaking the squire's hand. "All's well with him. No fear for a man that's been shot down in his duty to captain and owner."

Then he pulled me aside.

"Dr. Livesey," he said, "in how many weeks do you and squire expect the ship that Blandly was to send after us?"

I told him it would be not weeks but months. If we were not back by the end of August, Blandly was to send to find us, but neither sooner nor later. "You can figure for yourself," I said.

"Why, yes," returned the captain, scratching his head, "and I should say we were pretty badly off."

"How do you mean?" I asked.

"It's a pity, sir, we lost that second load. That's what I mean," replied the captain. "As for powder and shot, we'll do. But the food is short, very short—so short, Dr. Livesey, that we're perhaps as well without the extra mouth."

And he pointed to the dead body under the flag.

Just then, with a roar and a whistle, a shot from the ship's gun passed high above the roof of the log house and fell far beyond us in the wood.

"Oho!" said the captain. "Blaze away! You've little enough powder already, my lads."

At the second trial, the aim was better, and the ball fell inside the fence, scattering a cloud of sand, but doing no further damage.

"Captain," said the squire, "the house can't be seen from the ship. It must be the flag they are aiming at. Would it not be wiser to take it in?"

"Strike my colors!" cried the captain. "No, sir, not I!" And as soon as he said the words, I think we all agreed with him. For it was not only brave; it was a good idea besides, and showed our enemies that we cared nothing for their shots.

All through the evening they kept thundering away. Ball after ball flew over or fell short, or kicked up the sand near the fort. They had to fire so high that the shot fell dead and buried itself in the soft sand, and though one dropped in through the roof of the log house, no one minded them greatly.

"There is one thing good about all this," said the captain. "The woods in front of us is likely clear. The tide has been out a good while. The stores that sank with the jolly-boat should be above water. Who will go and bring in pork?"

Gray and Hunter were the first to come forward. Well-armed, they stole out of the fort, but it proved useless. The mutineers were bolder than we fancied, or they put more trust in Israel's big gun. For four or five of them were busy carrying off our stores and taking them out to one of the gigs that lay close by. Silver was in the stern, in command; and every man of them now had a gun from some secret hiding place of their own.

The captain sat down to his log,* and here is the beginning of his notes:

"Alexander Smollett, master; David Livesey, ship's doctor; Abraham Gray, carpenter's mate; John Trelawney, owner; John Hunter and Richard Joyce, owner's servants —being all that is left faithful of the ship's company—with stores for ten days, came ashore this day, and flew British colors on the log house in Treasure Island. Thomas Redruth, owner's servant, shot by the mutineers; James Hawkins, cabin boy—"

And at the same time I was wondering over poor Jim Hawkins's fate.

A shout on the land side.

"Somebody hailing us," said Hunter who was on guard.

"Doctor! Squire! Captain! Hello, Hunter, is that you?" came the cries.

And I ran to the door in time to see Jim Hawkins, safe and sound, come climbing over the fence.

---

*Log: a record of what takes place on a ship.

19 Jim Hawkins Goes on with the Story: The Men in the Fort

As soon as Ben Gunn saw the colors he came to a halt, held me by the arm, and sat down.

"Now," said he, "there's your friends, sure enough."

"Far more likely it's the mutineers," I answered.

"That!" he cried. "Why, in a place like this, where nobody comes but gentlemen of fortune—pirates I mean—Silver would fly the Jolly Roger, you don't make no doubt of that. The Jolly Roger is the pirates' flag. No, that's your friends. There's been blows, too, and I reckon your friends have had the best of it; and here they are ashore in the old fort, as was made years and years ago by Flint. Ah, he was the man with a good head, was Flint! Except that he drank too much rum, his match were never seen. He was afraid of none, not he; only Silver."

"Well," said I, "that may be so. All the more reason that I should hurry on to join my friends."

"No, mate," returned Ben, "not you. You're a good boy, or I'm mistaken; but you're only a boy, after all. Now Ben Gunn is clever. Nothing wouldn't bring me there, where you're going—nothing, till I see your squire, and gets it on his word of honor that he'll be generous with me. And you won't forget my words, will you?"

And he pinched me the third time with the same air of cleverness.

"And when Ben Gunn is wanted, you know where to find him, Jim. Just where you found him today. And him that comes to me is to have a white flag in his hand, and he's to come alone. Oh! and you'll say this: 'Ben Gunn,' you'll say, 'has reasons of his own.'"

"Well," said I, "I believe I understand. You want to make a bargain, and you wish to see the squire or the doctor; and you're to be found where I found you. Is that all?"

"And when?" he added. "Why, from about noon to about six."

"Good," said I, "and now may I go?"

"You won't forget?" he asked. "Well, then"—still holding me—"I guess you can go, Jim. And Jim, if you was to see Silver, you wouldn't tell on Ben Gunn? Wild horses wouldn't draw it from you? No, says you. And if them pirates camp ashore, Jim, what would you say if some of them were dead in the morning?"

Just then there was a loud report, and a cannon ball came tearing through the trees and pitched in the sand, not a hundred yards from where we two were talking. The next moment each of us had taken to his heels in a different direction.

For a good hour to come cannon balls kept crashing through the woods. I moved from hiding place to hiding place, always followed, it seemed to me, by these fearful shots. But after a while, though I still feared to go to the fort, where the shots fell most often, I crept down among the trees by the shore.

The sun had just set and the sea breeze was rustling and tumbling in the woods. The tide, too, was far out, and great patches of sand lay bare. The air, after the heat of the day, chilled me through my coat.

The *Hispaniola* still lay where she had anchored; but, sure enough, there was the Jolly Roger—the black flag of the pirates—flying from her peak. Even as I looked, there came another red flash and another shot that sent the echoes flying, and one more cannon ball whistled through the air. It was the last of them for the moment.

I lay for some time watching the pirates. They were chopping something with axes on the beach near the fort—the poor jolly-boat, I afterward learned. Down near the mouth of the river, a great fire was glowing among the trees. Between that point and the ship, one of the gigs kept coming and going. The men, whom I had seen so gloomy, were now shouting at the oars like children. But there was a sound in their voices which made me think they were drinking.

At length I thought I might return toward the fort. I was pretty far down on the low sandy point that lies to the east of the harbor. Now, as I rose to my feet, I saw a single rock, pretty high and an odd white in color. I thought that this might be the white rock of which Ben Gunn had spoken, and that some day or other a boat might be wanted and I should know where to look for one.

Then I walked back through the woods until I had come to the rear of the fort, and was soon warmly welcomed by the faithful party.

I had soon told my story, and began to look about me. The log house was made of pine—roof and walls. There was a thick layer of sand underfoot. There was a porch at the door, and under this porch was the little spring, bubbling up through the sand.

Little had been left beside the frame of the house. But in one corner there was a big flat stone laid down for a fireplace, and an iron basket to contain the fire.

The slopes of the hill and all the inside of the fort had been cleared of timber to build the house. We could see by the stumps what fine tall trees had been destroyed. Very close around the fort—too close for safety, they said—the woods were still high and thick, all of pine on the land side, but toward the sea a large number of oaks.

The cold evening breeze whistled through the building, and blew the sand up from the floor. There was sand in our eyes, sand in our teeth, sand in our suppers, and sand dancing at the bottom of the spring. Our chimney was a square hole in the roof. Only a little part of the smoke found its way out, and the rest floated about the house and kept us coughing and wiping our eyes.

Add to this that Gray, the new man, had his face tied up in a cloth for a cut he had got in breaking away from the mutineers. And poor old Tom Redruth, still not buried, lay along the wall under the flag.

If we had been allowed to sit idle, we should all have become gloomy, but Captain Smollett was never the man for that. All hands were called up before him, and he divided us into watches. The doctor and Gray and I, for one; the squire, Hunter, and Joyce for the other. Tired though we all were, two were sent out for wood for the fire; two more were set to dig a grave for Redruth. The doctor was named cook; I was the watch at the door; and the captain himself went from one to another, keeping up our spirits and lending a hand wherever it was wanted.

From time to time the doctor came to the door for a little air and to rest his eyes, which were almost smoked out of his head. Whenever he did so, he had a word for me.

"That man Smollett," he said once, "is a better man than I am. And when I say that it means a good deal, Jim."

Another time he came and was silent for a while. Then he put his head on one side and looked at me.

"Is this Ben Gunn a man?" he asked.

"I do not know, sir," said I. "I think he might be crazy."

"If there's any doubt about the matter, he is not," returned the doctor. "A man who has been three years all alone on a desert island, Jim, can't expect to seem the same as you or me. Was it cheese you said he had a fancy for?"

"Yes, sir, cheese," I answered.

"Well, Jim," says he, "just see the good that comes of being fond of good food. You remember the little box I have, don't you? Well, in that little box I carry a piece of cheese—a cheese made in Italy, very rich. Well, that's for Ben Gunn!"

Before supper was eaten we buried old Tom in the sand, and stood round him for a while bareheaded in the breeze. A good deal of wood had been got in, but not enough to suit the captain. He shook his head over it and told us we "must get back to this tomorrow rather more lively." Then, when we had eaten our pork, the three chiefs got together in a corner to talk things over.

It seems they were at their wits' end about what to do, as there was so little food that we should surely starve before help came. But our best hope, they thought, was to kill off the pirates until they either hauled down their flag or ran away with the *Hispaniola*. After the fight there were only 15 left of the 19; two others were wounded, and one at least—the man shot beside the gun—badly wounded, if he were not dead. Every time we had a crack at them, we were to take it, saving our own lives with the greatest of care. And, besides that, we had two friends—rum and the climate.

As for the rum, though we were about half a mile away, we could hear the pirates roaring and singing late into the night. As for the climate, the doctor was certain that, camped where they were in the marsh, the half of them would be on their backs with fever before a week.

"So," he added, "if we are not all shot down first, they'll be glad to leave in the *Hispaniola*. It's always a ship, and they can sail away as pirates, I suppose."

"First ship that ever I lost," said Captain Smollett.

I was dead tired, as you may fancy. When I got to sleep, which was not till after a great deal of tossing, I slept like a log.

The rest had long been up, and had already eaten breakfast and had brought in a great pile of wood, when I was wakened by a noise and the sound of voices.

"Flag of truce!" I heard someone say. Then immediately after, with a cry of surprise, "Silver himself!"

And at that, up I jumped and, rubbing my eyes, ran to an opening in the wall to see what was happening.

20 Silver's Message

Sure enough, there were two men just outside the fence, one of them waving a white cloth; the other, Silver himself, standing calmly by.

It was still quite early, and the coldest morning that I think I ever remember. The sky was bright and the tops of the trees shone in the sun. But where Silver stood with his man all was still in shadow, and they waded knee deep in a low white mist that had crawled during the night out of the swamp. The chill and the fog were proof that the island was damp, full of fever, and certainly not a healthful spot.

"Keep inside, men," said the captain. "Ten to one this is a trick."

Then he hailed Silver.

"Who goes? Stand, or we fire."

"Flag of truce," cried Silver.

The captain was in the porch, keeping himself carefully out of the way if a shot should be fired. He turned and spoke to us.

"Doctor, put your guards at their posts. Dr. Livesey take the north side, if you please; Jim, the east; Gray, west. The others stand by to load the guns. Lively, men, and careful."

And then he turned again to the mutineers.

"And what do you want with your flag of truce?" he cried.

This time it was the other man who replied.

"Cap'n Silver, sir, to come inside and make a bargain," he shouted.

"Cap'n Silver! Don't know him. Who's he?" cried the captain. And we could hear him adding to himself: "Cap'n, is it? Cap'n, indeed!"

Long John answered for himself.

"Me, sir. These poor lads have chosen me cap'n after you left, sir. We're willing to give up, if we can make a bargain, and no bones about it. All I ask is your word, Cap'n Smollett, to let me safe and sound out of this here fort, and one minute to get out of shot before a gun is fired."

"My man," said Captain Smollett, "I have not the least wish to talk to you. If you wish to talk to me, you can come, that's all. If there are any tricks, they'll be on your side, and the Lord help you."

"That's enough, cap'n," shouted Long John, cheerfully. "A word from you's enough. I know a gentleman, and you may lay to that."

We could see the man who carried the flag of truce trying to hold Silver back. But Silver laughed at him aloud, and slapped him on the back, as if the idea of fear were silly. Then he walked up to the fence, threw over his crutch, and with great strength and skill got himself over the fence and dropped safely to the other side.

I was far too much taken up with what was going on to be of any use as a guard. Indeed, I had already left my post and crept up behind the captain, who had now seated himself on the step, with his elbows on his knees, his head in his hands, and his eyes fixed on the water, as it bubbled out of the spring in the sand. He was whistling to himself, "Come, lasses and lads."

Silver had terrible hard work getting up the hill. What with the steep slope, the thick tree stumps, and the soft sand, he and his crutch were almost helpless. But he stuck to it like a man in silence, and at last stood before the captain, whom he greeted in great style. He was tricked out in his best. A huge blue coat hung to his knees and a fine hat was set on the back of his head.

"Here you are, my man," said the captain, raising his head. "You had better sit down."

"You ain't a-going to let me inside, cap'n?" asked Long John. "It's a cold morning, to be sure, sir, to sit outside upon the sand."

"Why, Silver," said the captain, "if you had pleased to be an honest man, you might have been sitting in your galley. It's your own doing. You're either my ship's cook—and then you were treated well—or Cap'n Silver, a common mutineer and pirate, and then you can go hang!"

"Well, well, cap'n," returned the sea cook, sitting down as he was told on the sand, "you'll have to give me a hand to help me up again, that's all. A sweet pretty place you have of it here. Ah, there's Jim! The top of the morning to you, Jim.—Doctor, you, too. Why, there you all are together like a happy family."

"If you have anything to say, my man, better say it," said the captain.

"Right you were, Cap'n Smollett," replied Silver. "Duty is duty, to be sure. Well now, you look here, that was a good trick of yours last night. I don't deny it was a good trick. Some of you are pretty handy with a club. And I'll not deny neither but what some of my people was scared—maybe all was scared. Maybe I was scared myself. Maybe that's why I'm here to bargain. But you mark me, cap'n, it don't do twice, by thunder!

We'll have to keep a guard and drink a little less rum. Maybe you think we all had too much rum last night. But I'll tell you I was sober; I was only dog-tired. And if I'd woke a second sooner I'd have caught you in the act, I would. He wasn't dead when I got round to him, not he."

"Well?" says Captain Smollett, as cool as can be.

All that Silver said was a puzzle to the captain, but you would never have guessed it from his tone. As for me, I began to have an idea what it was all about. Gunn's last words came back to my mind. I began to see that he had paid the mutineers a visit while they all lay drunk together round their fire, and I knew that now we had only 14 enemies to deal with.

"Well, here it is," said Silver. "We want that treasure—and we'll have it—that's our point! You would just as soon save your lives, I guess; and that's yours. You have a chart, haven't you?"

"That's as may be," replied the captain.

"Oh, well, you have, I know that," returned Long John. "You needn't be so short with a man. There ain't a bit of use in that, and you may lay to it. What I mean is, we want your chart. Now, I never meant you no harm, myself."

"That won't do with me, my man," cried the captain. "We know exactly what you meant to do, and we don't care; for now, you see, you can't do it."

And the captain looked at him calmly, and began to fill a pipe.

"If Abe Gray—" Silver broke out.

"Stop right there!" cried Captain Smollett. "Gray told me nothing; and I asked him nothing. And I would see you and him and this whole island blown clean out of the water first. So that's what I think about that, my man."

This little burst of temper seemed to cool Silver down. He had been growing angry before, but now he pulled himself together.

"Like enough," said he. "And, seeing as how you are about to smoke a pipe, cap'n, I'll make so free as to do the same."

And he filled a pipe and lighted it. The two men sat silently smoking for quite a while, now looking each other in the face, now leaning forward to spit. It was as good as a play to see them.

"Now," went on Silver, "here it is. You give us the chart to get the treasure by, and stop shooting poor seamen, and clubbing in their heads while they're asleep. You do that, and we'll offer you a choice. You can come aboard with us when the treasure is loaded, and then I'll give you my promise, upon my word of honor, to put you somewhere safe ashore. Or, if that ain't to your fancy, some of my men being rough, then you can stay here, you can. We'll divide stores with you, man for man. I'll give my promise, as before, to speak to the first ship I sight and send them here to pick you up. Now you know that's fair. You couldn't do better. And I hope"—raising his voice—"that all hands in this here blockhouse will hear my words, for what is spoke to one is spoke to all."

Captain Smollett rose from his seat, and knocked out the ashes of his pipe in the palm of his left hand.

"Is that all?" he asked.

"Every last word, by thunder!" answered John. "Refuse that, and you've seen the last of me except shots from my gun."

"Very good," said the captain. "Now you'll hear me. If you'll come up one by one, I'll put you all in irons, and take you home to a fair trial in England. If you won't, my name is Alexander Smollett, I've served my king, and I'll make no deal with you. You can't find the treasure. You can't sail the ship—there's not a man among you fit to sail the ship. You can't fight us— Gray, there, got away from five of you. I stand here and tell you so; and they're the last good words you'll get from me. For, in the name of heaven, I'll put a bullet in you when next I meet you. Tramp, my lad. Get out of this, please, and double quick."

Silver's face was a picture; his eyes started in his head with anger. He shook the fire out of his pipe.

"Give me a hand up!" he cried.

"Not I," returned the captain.

"Who'll give me a hand up?" he roared.

Not a man among us moved. Growling and cursing, he crawled along the sand till he got hold of the porch and could lift himself again upon his crutch. Then he spat into the spring.

"There!" he cried, "that's what I think of you. Before an hour's out, I'll shoot your old blockhouse to pieces like nothing. Laugh, by thunder, laugh! Before an hour's out, you'll laugh on the other side. Them that die will be the lucky ones."

And with a dreadful oath he stumbled off, down through the sand, was helped across the fence by the man with the flag of truce, and disappeared among the trees.

21 *The Attack*

As soon as Silver left, the captain, who had been closely watching him, came into the house, and found not a man of us at his post but Gray. It was the first time we had ever seen him angry.

"To your posts!" he roared. And then, as we all flew back to our places, "Gray," he said, "I'll put your name in the log; you've stood by your duty like a seaman. Mr. Trelawney, I'm surprised at you, sir. Doctor, I thought better of you!"

The watch all went back at their posts. The rest were busy loading the spare guns, every one with a red face, you may be sure.

The captain looked on for a while in silence. Then he spoke.

"My lads," said he, "I've given Silver our answer, and before the hour's out, as he said, we shall be attacked. They have more men than we have, I needn't tell you that; but we fight from behind walls, and they must fight in the open. I think that we can beat them, if you choose."

Then he went the rounds and saw, as he said, that all was clear.

On the two short sides of the house, east and west, there were only two openings; on the south side where the porch was, two again; and on the north side, five. There were 20 guns for the seven of us. The wood had been built into four piles—tables, you might say—one about the middle of each side. On each of these tables some powder and shot and four loaded guns were laid ready for our use. The cutlasses lay in the middle.

"Put out the fire," said the captain. "The chill is past, and we mustn't have smoke in our eyes."

The iron fire basket was carried out by Mr. Trelawney, and the coals covered with sand.

"Hawkins hasn't had his breakfast. Hawkins, help yourself, and back to your post to eat it," said Captain Smollett. "Lively now, my lad. You'll want it before you've done. Hunter, serve out a round of rum to all hands."

And while this was going on, the captain finished, in his own mind, the plan of battle.

"Doctor, you will take the door," he went on. "See, but don't show yourself. Keep inside and fire through the porch. Hunter, take the east side, there. Joyce, you stand by the west, my man. Mr. Trelawney, you are the best shot—you and Gray will take this long north side, with the five openings; it's there the danger is. If they can get up to it and fire in upon us through our own openings, things would begin to look bad. Hawkins, neither you nor I are much good at the shooting. We'll stand by to load the guns and help where we can."

As the captain had said, the chill was past. As soon as the sun had climbed above the trees, it quickly drank up the fog. Soon the sand was baking. Coats were flung aside, shirts thrown open at the neck and rolled up to the shoulders; and we stood there, each at his post, in a fever of heat and fear.

An hour passed away.

"Hang them!" said the captain. "This is dull! Gray, whistle for a wind."

And just at that moment came the first news of the attack.

"If you please, sir," said Joyce, "if I see anyone am I to fire?"

"I told you so!" cried the captain.

"Thank you, sir," returned Joyce, quietly.

Nothing followed for a time, but his words had set us all watching and straining ears and eyes. The men had their guns in their hands, and the captain stood out in the middle of the blockhouse, with his mouth very tight and a frown on his face.

So some seconds passed, till suddenly Joyce whipped up his gun and fired. The sound had scarcely died away before it was repeated and repeated from outside, shot after shot, like a string of geese, from every side of the fort. Several bullets struck the log house, but not one came inside. As the smoke cleared away, the fort and the woods around it looked as quiet and empty as before. Not a bough waved, not the gleam of a gun barrel told us where our enemies were.

"Did you hit your man?" asked the captain.

"No, sir," replied Joyce. "I believe not, sir."

"Next best thing to tell the truth," muttered Captain Smollett. "Load his gun, Hawkins. How many do you think there were on your side, doctor?"

"I know exactly," said Dr. Livesey. "Three shots were fired on this side. I saw the three flashes—two close together—one farther to the west."

"Three!" cried the captain. "And how many on yours, Mr. Trelawney?"

But this was not so easily answered. There had come many from the north—seven, by the squire's count, eight or nine, thought Gray. From the east and west only a single shot had been fired. It was plain, therefore, that the main attack would come from the north. But Captain Smollett made no change in his plans. If the mutineers should be able to cross the fence and get as far as the blockhouse, they could easily reach the openings and shoot us down like rats in our own fort.

We had not much time left to us for thought. Suddenly, with a loud shout, a little group of pirates leaped from the woods on the north side and ran straight toward the fence. At the same moment, those in the woods began to fire. A rifle ball sang through the doorway and knocked the doctor's gun into bits.

The pirates swarmed over the fence like monkeys. Squire and Gray fired again and yet again. Three men fell, one forward inside the fence, two back on the outside. But of these, one seemed to be more frightened than hurt, for he was on his feet again in a hurry, and quickly ran back among the trees.

Two had bit the dust, one had fled, four were inside our fence; while from the woods seven or eight men kept up a hot though useless fire on the log house.

The four who had come inside the fence made straight for the building, shouting as they ran. Several shots were fired. But, such was the hurry of the pirates, not one shot did any harm. In a moment, the four men had swarmed up the hill and were upon us.

The head of Job Anderson appeared at the middle opening.

"At 'em, all hands—all hands!" he roared, in a voice of thunder.

At the same moment, another pirate grasped Hunter's gun, tore it from his hands, pulled it through the opening, and, with a heavy blow, knocked the poor fellow to the floor. Meanwhile a third, running all round the house, appeared suddenly in the doorway and attacked the doctor with his cutlass. A moment ago we were firing under cover at an enemy in the open. Now it was we who were uncovered, and could not return a blow.

The log house was full of smoke, and the pirates could not see just where we stood. Shouts, the flashes and sounds of pistol shots, and one loud groan rang in my ears.

"Out, lads, out, and fight them in the open! Cutlasses!" cried the captain.

I snatched a cutlass from the pile, and someone, at the same time snatching another, gave me a cut across the fingers which I hardly felt. I dashed out of the door into the clear sunlight. Someone was close behind, I knew not whom. Right in front, the doctor was running after a man down the hill, and, just as my eyes fell upon him, struck him and sent him down on his back, with a great cut across his face.

"Round the house, lads! Round the house!" cried the captain; and even in the mix-up I heard a change in his voice.

I obeyed, turned eastward, and with my cutlass raised, ran round the corner of the house. Next moment I was face to face with Anderson. He roared aloud, and his cutlass went up above his head, flashing in the sunlight. I did not have time to be afraid, but, before he could strike me, I leaped to one side, and missing my step in the soft sand, rolled down the slope.

When I had first come out the door, the other mutineers had been already swarming up to make an end of us. One man in a red nightcap, with his cutlass in his mouth, had even got upon the top of the fence and thrown a leg across. Well, everything happened so quickly that when I found my feet again the fellow with the red nightcap was half way over the fence, and

another was just showing his head above the top. And yet, in this breath of time, the fight was over, and the victory was ours.

Gray, who was close behind me, had cut down big Job Anderson before he had time to turn. Another had been shot at an opening in the very act of firing into the house, and now lay in pain, the pistol still smoking in his hand. A third, the doctor finished at a blow. Of the four who had crossed the fence, only one escaped, and he was now climbing out again, leaving his cutlass behind him.

In three seconds nothing remained of the attacking party but the five who had fallen, four on the inside, and one on the outside of the fence.

The doctor and Gray and I ran full speed for the fort. The rest of the pirates would soon be back where they had left their guns, and at any moment the firing might begin again.

The house was by this time somewhat cleared of smoke, and we saw at a glance how things stood. Hunter lay beside his opening badly hurt. Joyce lay by his, shot through the head, never to move again; while right in the center, the squire was helping the captain, one as pale as the other.

"The captain's wounded," said Mr. Trelawney.

"Have they run?" asked Captain Smollett.

"All that could, you may be sure," returned the doctor, "but there's five of them will never run again."

"Five!" cried the captain. "Come, that's better. Five of their men and only three of ours. That leaves us four men to their nine. That's better odds than we had at the start. We were seven to nineteen then, or thought we were, and that's as bad to bear."*

---

* The mutineers were soon only eight in number, for the man shot by Mr. Trelawney on board the *Hispaniola* died that same evening of his wound. But this, of course, we did not know till afterward.

Book 5

My Sea Adventure

22 *How My Sea Adventure Began*

There was no return of the mutineers—not another shot out of the woods. They had "got enough for that day," as the captain put it, and we had the place to ourselves and a quiet time to look after the wounded and get dinner. Squire and I cooked outside in spite of the danger, and even there we could hardly tell what we were at, for horror of the loud groans that reached us from the doctor's patients.

Out of the eight men who had fallen in the battle, only three still breathed—one of the pirates, Hunter, and Captain Smollett. The first two of these were as good as dead and the pirate, indeed, died later. Hunter lived all day, breathing loudly like the old captain at home at the "Admiral Benbow." But sometime in the following night he died, without sign or sound.

As for the captain, his wounds were bad indeed but not dangerous. He was sure to get well, the doctor said, but in the meantime and for weeks to come, he must not walk nor move his arm, nor so much as speak when he could help it.

My own cut across the fingers was small. Dr. Livesey patched it up, and pulled my ears for me into the bargain.

After dinner the squire and the doctor sat by the captain's side a while talking. Then the doctor picked up his hat and pistols, took a cutlass, put the chart in his pocket, and with a gun over his shoulder, crossed the fence on the north side and set off rapidly through the trees.

Gray and I were sitting together at the far end of the blockhouse, to be out of hearing of our officers talking. Gray took his pipe out of his mouth and quite forgot to put it back again, so thunderstruck was he at the sight.

"Why, in the name of Davy Jones," said he, "is Dr. Livesey crazy?"

"Why, no," says I. "He's about the last of this crew for that, I think."

"Well, shipmate," said Gray, "he may not be crazy; but if *he's* not, you mark my words, *I* am."

"I think," replied I, "the doctor has an idea; and if I am right, he's going now to see Ben Gunn."

I was right, as we found later. But, in the meantime, the house being hot, and the little patch of sand inside the fence bright with the sun, I began to get another thought into my head, which was not by any means so right. What I began to do was to envy the doctor, walking in the cool shadow of the woods, with the birds about him and the pleasant smell of the pines; while I sat in the hot blockhouse, with so much blood about me and so many poor dead bodies lying all around.

All the time I was washing out the blockhouse, and then washing up the things from dinner, this envy kept growing stronger and stronger. At last, being near a bread bag, and no one seeing me, I filled both pockets of my coat with bread.

I was a fool, if you like, and certainly I was going to do a foolish, bold act; but I made up my mind to do it as carefully as I possibly could. This bread, if anything should happen to me, would keep me from starving till far on in the next day.

The next thing I took was a pair of pistols, and as I already had powder and bullets, I was well supplied with arms.

As for the plan I had in my head, it was not a bad one in itself. I meant to go down the sandy point that divides the harbor on the east from the open sea, find the white rock I had seen last evening, and see whether or not it was there that Ben Gunn had hidden his boat. But as I was sure I should not be allowed to leave the fort, my only plan was to slip out when nobody was watching. Of course, it was wrong to do it that way, but I was only a boy, and I had made up my mind.

Well, as things at last happened, I found a good chance to slip away. The squire and Gray were busy helping the captain with his wounds. The coast was clear. I made a dash for it over the fence and into the thickest of the trees.

I made my way straight for the east coast of the island, for I wished to go down the sea side of the sand point, so as not to be seen from the harbor. It was already late in the afternoon, although still warm and sunny. As I walked through the tall woods I could hear from far before me not only the thunder of the waves, but the sound of the rising wind in the trees. Soon cool breezes began to reach me. A few steps farther I came out to the edge of the woods, and saw the sea lying blue and sunny, and the waves tumbling and tossing their foam along the beach.

I have never seen the sea quiet round Treasure Island. The sun might blaze overhead, the air be still, the surface smooth and blue, but still these great waves would be running along the coast, thundering and thundering by day and night. I do not believe there is one spot in the island where a man would be out of hearing of their noise.

I walked along beside the sea, till, thinking I was now far enough to the south, I kept myself hidden behind some thick bushes and crept softly up to the ridge of the point.

Behind me was the sea; in front, the harbor. The surface lay as still and smooth as when we first saw it. The *Hispaniola*, in that smooth water, was reflected from the top of the mast to the water line, the Jolly Roger hanging from her peak.

Alongside lay one of the gigs, Silver in the stern —I always knew him—while a couple of men were leaning over the stern rail. One of them wore a red cap—the very rascal that I had seen some hours before, crossing the fence. They seemed to be talking and laughing, though at that distance—almost a mile—I could not hear a word of what was said. All at once, there began the most horrid, wild screaming, which at first startled me badly. But I soon remembered the voice of Silver's parrot, Captain Flint, and even thought I could make out the bird by her bright feathers as she sat perched upon her master's shoulder.

Soon after, the jolly-boat moved away and pulled for shore, and the man with the red cap and his comrade went below by the cabin stairs.

Just about the same time the sun went down behind the Spyglass, and the fog rose rapidly. It began to grow dark in earnest. I saw I must lose no time if I were to find the boat that evening.

The white rock was still an eighth of a mile farther down the point. It took me a good while to get to it, crawling often on all fours among the bushes. Night had almost come when I laid my hand on its rough sides. Right below it there was a tiny hollow of green grass; and in the center, sure enough, there was a little tent of goatskins.

I dropped into the hollow, lifted the side of the tent, and there was Ben Gunn's boat—homemade if ever anything was homemade. It was a rough frame of

wood with a covering of goatskin stretched upon it, with the hair inside. The thing was extremely small, even for me, and I can not imagine that it could have floated with a grown man. There was one seat set as low as possible, and a double paddle.

Well, now that I had found the boat, you would think I would have returned to the fort; but I had taken another notion. This was to slip out at night, cut the *Hispaniola* loose, and let her go ashore wherever she drifted. I thought that the mutineers, after their defeat of the morning, might lift the anchor and sail away. It seemed to me that it would be a fine thing to stop this. Now that I saw how they left their watchmen without a small boat, I thought it might be done with little risk.

I sat down to wait for darkness and ate my bread. It was a perfect night for my purpose. The fog was now very thick. As the last rays of daylight disappeared, blackness settled down on Treasure Island. And when at last I lifted the small boat and made my way out of the hollow where I had eaten, there were only two points to be seen on the whole harbor.

One was the great fire on shore, by which the defeated pirates were drinking in the swamp. The other, a patch of light upon the darkness, showed where the anchored ship lay. She had swung round with the tide and her bow was now toward me; the only lights on board were in the cabin. What I saw was merely a glow on the fog of the strong light from the stern window.

The tide had already run out some time, and I had to wade through a long strip of swampy sand before I came to the edge of the water. Wading a little way in, I set my boat on the surface of the harbor.

23 The Tide Runs Out

The boat was a very safe one for a person of my size. She rode lightly on the water, but she was extremely hard to handle. Do as you pleased, she always moved to the side more than anything else, and turning round and round was what she was best at. Even Ben Gunn himself said that she was "queer to handle till you knew her way."

Certainly I did not know her way. She turned in every direction but the one I wished to go. The most part of the time we were going to one side, and I am very sure I never should have got to the ship at all except for the tide. By good fortune, paddle as I pleased, the tide was still sweeping me down; and there lay the *Hispaniola* right in the way, hardly to be missed.

First she loomed before me like a patch of something yet blacker than darkness. Then she began to take shape. The next moment, as it seemed (for the further I went, the swifter grew the current of the tide), I was beside her and had seized in my hands the thick rope which held her to the anchor.

The rope was stretched tight, and the current was so strong she pulled upon her anchor. All round her in the blackness, the rippling current bubbled and chattered like a little mountain stream. One cut with my sea knife, and the *Hispaniola* would move easily along with the tide.

So far so good. But I remembered that a tightly stretched rope, suddenly cut, is a thing as dangerous as a kicking horse. Ten to one, if I were so foolish as to cut the *Hispaniola* from her anchor, I and the boat would be knocked clean out of the water.

This brought me to a full stop, and if good luck had not come my way, I should have given up my plan. But the light breezes which had begun blowing from the southeast and south had swung round after night into the southwest. Just while I was thinking, a puff came, caught the *Hispaniola,* and forced her up against the current. To my great joy, I felt the rope loosen, and my hand dipped for a second under water.

With that I made up my mind, took out my knife, opened it with my teeth, and cut almost through the heavy rope, leaving just enough to hold the vessel. Then I lay quiet, waiting to cut the rest of it when the wind should again loosen the rope.

All this time I had heard the sound of loud voices from the cabin. But to tell the truth, my mind had been so taken up with other thoughts that I had scarcely listened. Now, however, when I had nothing else to do, I began to pay attention.

One voice I knew to be Israel Hands's, the man that had been Flint's gunner in former days. The other was, of course, my friend with the red nightcap. Both men were plainly the worse for drink, and they were still drinking. Even while I was listening, one of them, with a drunken cry, opened the stern window and threw out an empty bottle. But they were not only drinking; it was plain that they were extremely angry. Oaths flew like hail, and every now and then there was such a burst of anger that I thought the men would surely come to blows. But each time the quarrel passed off, and the voices grumbled lower for a while until the next time, when it began all over again.

On shore, I could see the glow of the great camp fire burning warmly through the trees. Someone was singing a dull, old, sailor's song, with a sad droop at the end of every verse and evidently no end to it at all. I had heard it on the voyage more than once, and remembered these words:

> "But one man of her crew alive,
> What put to sea with seventy-five."

And I thought it was a song fit for a company that had met such cruel losses in the morning. But, indeed, from what I saw, all these pirates were as hard-hearted as the sea they sailed on.

At last the breeze came; the schooner slid to one side and drew nearer in the dark. I felt the rope loosen once more, and with a good strong effort, cut through the last thickness.

I was almost instantly swept against the bows of the *Hispaniola*. At the same time the schooner began to turn upon her heel, swinging slowly end for end across the current.

I paddled like mad, for I expected every moment to be sunk; and since I found I could not push the boat directly off, I now pushed straight back. At length I was clear of my dangerous neighbor. Just as I gave the last push, my hands came across a light rope that was trailing overboard from the stern of the ship. Instantly I grasped it.

Why I did so I do not know. But as soon as I had it in my hands and found it fastened firmly to the ship, I decided to have one look through the cabin window.

I pulled in hand over hand on the rope and, when I thought myself near enough, stood up in the boat at great risk so that I could see the roof and the inside of the cabin.

By this time the schooner and my little boat beside her were gliding pretty swiftly through the water. Indeed, we were already opposite the camp fire. The ship was talking loudly, as the sailors say—that is, the ripples were splashing against her as she swept across the harbor. Until I looked into the window I could not understand why the two men had not noticed that the ship was moving. One glance, however, was enough. It showed me Hands and his companion locked together in a deadly fight, each with a hand upon the other's throat.

I dropped upon the seat again, none too soon, for my little boat nearly turned over. I could see nothing for the moment but those two furious red faces, swaying together under the smoky lamp. And I shut my eyes to let them grow once more used to the darkness.

The endless song had come to an end at last, and the pirates around the camp fire had broken into the chorus I had heard so often:

> "Fifteen men on the dead man's chest—
> Yo-ho-ho, and a bottle of rum!
> Drink and the devil had done for the rest—
> Yo-ho-ho, and a bottle of rum!"

I was just thinking how busy drink and the devil were at that very moment in the cabin of the *Hispaniola,* when I was surprised by a sudden rolling of my boat. At the same moment she swung sharply and seemed to change her course and to move strangely faster.

I opened my eyes at once. All round me were little ripples, bubbling over with a light, sharp sound. The *Hispaniola* seemed to stagger in her course. I saw her mast toss a little against the blackness of the night. As I looked longer, I saw that she also was swinging to the southward. All this time, I was being whirled along behind her by the current.

I glanced over my shoulder, and my heart jumped against my ribs. There, right behind me, was the glow of the camp fire. The current had turned at right angles, carrying along with it the tall schooner and my little dancing boat. For, moving faster and faster, the current was sweeping us through the narrow straits toward the open sea.

Suddenly the schooner in front of me gave a violent turn, swinging perhaps through 20 degrees. Almost at the same moment one shout followed another from on board. I could hear feet pounding on the ladder, and I knew that the two fighters had been interrupted in their quarrel and at last knew of their danger.

I lay down flat in the bottom of that wretched boat, and prayed. At the end of the straits, I knew we must come into the line of the huge waves which break along the shore, where all my troubles would be ended quickly. And though I could perhaps bear to die, I could not bear to see my fate as it came.

So I must have lain for hours, beaten to and fro upon the waves, and always expecting death at the next moment. Gradually I grew weary, until sleep at last came, and in my sea-tossed boat I lay and dreamed of home and the old "Admiral Benbow."

24 *The Cruise of the Small Boat*

It was broad day when I awoke, and found myself tossing at the southwest end of Treasure Island. The sun was up, but was still hidden from me behind the Spyglass, the highest of the hills, which on this side dropped off almost to the sea in steep cliffs.

Nearby were Haulbowline Head and Mizzenmast Hill. The hill was bare and dark, with cliffs 40 or 50 feet high, and covered with great masses of fallen rock. I was not more than a quarter of a mile out to sea, and it was my first thought to paddle in and land.

That notion was soon given up. Among the fallen rocks the great waves pounded and roared. I could see that if I tried to land, I should be dashed to death upon the rough shore.

Nor was that all. For crawling together on flat tables of rock or letting themselves drop into the sea with great splashes, I saw huge smooth monsters, dozens of them together, making the rocks echo with their barking.

I now know that they were sea lions,* and entirely harmless. But the look of them frightened me, and I felt willing rather to starve at sea than to face such dangers.

In the meantime, I had a better chance, as I thought, before me. North of Haulbowline Head, the land runs in a long way, leaving a long stretch of yellow sand at low tide. To the north of that, there is another point—Cape of the Woods, as it was called upon the chart.

* Sea Lion: any of several large-eared seals.

I remembered what Silver had said about the current that runs northward along the whole west coast of Treasure Island. Seeing that I was already in it, I decided to leave Haulbowline Head behind me, and save my strength to try to land upon the Cape of the Woods.

There was a great smooth swell upon the sea. As both the wind and the current were from the south, the waves were not rough but rose and fell smoothly.

Had this not been the case, I should long ago have been drowned. But, as it was, it is surprising how easily and safely my little light boat could ride. Often, as I still lay at the bottom and kept no more than an eye above the edge, I would see the big blue top of a wave close above me. Yet, the boat would only bounce a little, dance as if on springs, and slide around the other side of the wave as lightly as a bird.

I began after a little to grow very bold, and sat up to try my skill at paddling. But even a small change in my position caused sharp changes in the movements of the boat. And I had hardly moved before the boat, giving up at once her gentle dancing movement, ran straight down a steep slope of water and struck her nose deep into the side of the next wave.

I was soaked and terrified, and fell instantly back into the bottom. At once the boat seemed to find her head again, and led me as softly as before among the waves. It was plain I must let her alone. At that rate, since I could not steer her, how could I hope to reach land?

I began to be horribly frightened, but I kept my head, for all that. First, moving with all care, I gradually dipped the water out of the boat with my cap. Then I got my eye once more above the edge, and set myself to study how it was she could slip so quietly through the waves.

I found each wave, instead of the big smooth mountain it looks from the shore, or from a vessel's deck, was for all the world like any range of hills on the dry land, full of peaks and smooth places and valleys. The boat, left to herself, turning from side to side, found her way through these lower parts, and did not climb the steep slopes of the waves.

"Well, now," thought I to myself, "it is plain I must lie where I am, and not disturb her balance. But I can put the paddle over the side, and from time to time, give her a push or two toward land." No sooner thought than done. There I lay on my elbows, and every now and again giving a weak stroke or two to turn her toward shore.

It was very hard, slow work, yet I did manage to go some distance nearer shore. But I saw that I should miss the Cape of the Woods. I was, indeed, close in. I could see the cool green treetops swaying together in the breeze, and I felt sure I should make the next point without fail.

It was high time, for I now began to be thirsty. The glow of the sun from above and the sea water that fell and dried upon me, covering my very lips with salt, made my throat burn and my brain ache. The sight of the trees so near at hand almost made me sick with longing, but the current soon carried me past the point. As I passed the Cape of the Woods, I saw a sight that changed my thoughts completely.

Right in front of me, not half a mile away, I saw the *Hispaniola* under sail. I was sure, of course, that the men on board would catch me, but I was so thirsty that I scarcely knew whether to be glad or sorry at the thought. Long before I had made up my mind about it, I was so surprised at what I saw that I could do nothing but stare and wonder.

The *Hispaniola* was under her mainsail and two jibs, or smaller sails, and the beautiful white canvas shone in the sun like snow or silver. When I first saw her, all her sails were drawing. She was lying a course about northwest, and I believed the men on board were going round the island on their way back to the harbor. Soon she began to move more and more to the westward, so that I thought they had seen me and were going to chase me. At last, however, she fell right into the wind's eye, stopped short, and stood there a while helpless, with her sails shivering.

"Clumsy fellows," said I, "they must still be drunk as owls." And I thought how Captain Smollett would have sent them flying.

Meanwhile, the schooner gradually moved around, her sails filled again, and she was off upon another flight. She sailed swiftly for a minute or so, and brought up once more dead in the wind's eye. This happened again and again. To and fro, up and down, north, south, east and west, the *Hispaniola* sailed by darts and dashes. Each time she ended as she had begun, with idly flapping sails. It became plain to me that nobody was steering. And, if so, where were the men? Either they were dead drunk or had deserted her, I thought. Perhaps if I could get on board, I might return the vessel to her captain.

The current was carrying my boat and the schooner southward at the same speed. If only I dared to sit up and paddle, I was sure that I could overtake her. There was an air of adventure about it that pleased me, and the thought of the drinking water on board gave me courage.

Up I got, and in spite of the dash of water which greeted me, I stuck to my plan. I set myself, with all my strength, to paddle after the *Hispaniola*. Once so much water ran into the boat that I had to stop and dip it out, with my heart fluttering like a bird. Gradually I learned the trick of guiding her among the waves, with only now and then a blow upon her bows and a dash of foam in my face.

I was now gaining rapidly on the schooner. Still no one appeared upon her decks. I began to think she was deserted. If not, the men were lying drunk below, where I might lock them down, perhaps, and do what I chose with the ship.

For some time she had been doing the worst thing possible for me—standing still. Each time she fell off her sails partly filled, and these brought her, in a moment, right to the wind again. I have said this was the worst thing possible for me. For helpless as she looked, with her canvas cracking like cannon, she still continued to run away from me.

But at last I had my chance. The breeze fell, for some seconds, very low. The current gradually turned the *Hispaniola* slowly round her center, until at last the stern of the ship came round in front of me. The cabin window was still open, and the lamp over the table still burned on into the day. The mainsail hung drooped like a banner. She was standing still and now I began once more to gain on her.

I was not a hundred yards from her when the wind came again in a rush. She filled and was off again, stooping and skimming like a swallow.

Round she came, toward me—round still till she had covered a half, then two-thirds, and then three-quarters of the distance between us. I could see the waves boiling white under her foot. Immensely tall she looked to me from my place low in the little boat.

And then, suddenly, I began to understand my danger. I scarcely had time to think—scarcely had time to act and save myself. I was on the top of one wave when the schooner came sweeping over the next. I saw that the pole which points forward at the front of the schooner was right over my head. I sprang to my feet and caught it, pushing my small boat under water. As I clung there out of breath, a dull blow told me that the schooner had run down my boat. I was left on the *Hispaniola* with no means of escape.

25 *I Strike the Jolly Roger*

The wind filled the sails suddenly, causing the ship to tremble and nearly tossing me back into the sea. So now I lost no time but tumbled head first onto the deck.

The mainsail, which was still drawing, hid from me a part of the afterdeck.* Not a soul was to be seen. The deck, which had not been washed since the mutiny, was covered with the marks of many feet. An empty bottle broken by the neck, tumbled to and fro with the movement of the ship.

Suddenly the *Hispaniola* came right into the wind. The sails behind me cracked aloud. The whole ship trembled, and at the same moment the mainsail swung across the deck and showed me the afterdeck.

There were the two watchmen, sure enough. Red-cap lay on his back, as stiff as a board, with his arms stretched out like a cross, and his teeth showing through his open lips. Israel Hands sat propped against the side, his chin on his chest, his hands lying open before him on the deck, his face deathly white.

For a while the ship kept buckling like a wild horse, now sailing one direction, now another. At every jump of the schooner, Red-cap slipped to and fro. It was awful to see that, in rolling about the deck, his arms remained stretched out as before, and he still showed his teeth in that horrible grin. At every jump, too, Hands seemed to sink still more into himself and

---

*Afterdeck: the part of the deck in the middle section of a ship.

settle down upon the deck. His feet slipped ever farther out, and his whole body leaned away from me, so that his face became, little by little hid from me. At last I could see nothing but his ear.

At the same time, I noticed, around both of them, splashes of dark blood upon the deck, and I began to feel sure that they had killed each other in their drunken anger.

While I was thus looking, Israel Hands turned partly round and, with a low groan, raised himself back to the position in which I had seen him first. The groan, which told of pain and weakness, and the way in which his jaw hung open, went right to my heart. But when I remembered the talk I had overheard from the apple barrel, all pity left me.

I walked back until I reached the mainmast.

"Come aboard, Mr. Hands," I said.

He rolled his eyes round heavily; but he was too far gone to show surprise. All he could do was to speak one word, "Rum."

There was no time to lose. Dodging the sail as it once more swung across the deck, I slipped back and down the stairs into the cabin.

All the locked places had been broken open in search of the chart. The floor was thick with mud, where the pirates had sat down to drink or talk after wading in the marshes round their camp. The walls, all painted in clear white and trimmed round with gold, were covered with the marks of dirty hands. Dozens of empty bottles clattered together in corners to the rolling of the ship. One of the doctor's books lay open on the table, half of the leaves torn out, I suppose, to light their pipes. In the midst of all this the lamp still cast a smoky glow.

I went into the cellar. All the barrels were gone, and a great number of the bottles had been drunk empty and thrown away. Certainly, since the mutiny began, not a man of them could ever have been sober.

Looking around, I found a bottle with some rum left, for Hands; and for myself some bread and a piece of cheese. With these I came on deck and put down my own stock well out of Israel's reach. I then went forward to the water barrel and had a good, deep drink of water, and then, and not till then, gave Hands the rum.

He must have drunk most of it before he took the bottle from his mouth.

"Ay," said he, "by thunder, but I wanted some of that!"

I had sat down already in my own corner and begun to eat.

"Much hurt?" I asked him.

"If that doctor was aboard," he said, "I'd be all right soon enough. But I don't have no luck, you see, and that's what is the matter with me. As for that man, he's good and dead, he is," he added, pointing to the man with the red cap. "He wasn't a good seaman, anyhow. And where might you have come from?"

"Well," said I, "I've come aboard to take charge of this ship, Mr. Hands. And you'll please call me your captain."

He looked at me darkly enough, but said nothing. Some of the color had come back into his cheeks, though he still looked very sick and still slipped every time the ship rolled.

"And," I added, "I can't have these colors, Mr. Hands; and, by your leave, I'll strike them. Better none than the Jolly Roger."

And again dodging the mainsail, I ran to the color lines, pulled down the hated black flag of the pirates, and threw it into the sea.

"God save the king!" said I, waving my cap. "And there's an end to Captain Silver!"

He watched me closely, his chin all the while on his chest.

"I guess," he said at last—"I guess, Cap'n Hawkins, you'll be wanting to get ashore, now. Suppose we make a bargain."

"Why, yes," says I, "with all my heart, Mr. Hands. Say on." And I went back to my meal.

"This man," he began, pointing to Red-cap—"O'Brien were his name—this man and me got the sails upon her, meaning for to sail her back. Well, *he's* dead now, he is; and who's to sail this ship? Unless I gives you a hint, *you* can't do it. Now, look here, you gives me food and drink and an old cloth to tie my wound up, you do; and I'll tell you how to sail her. And that's about square all round, I think."

"I'll tell you one thing," says I. "I'm not going back to Captain Kidd's harbor. I mean to get into North Inlet, and beach her there."

"To be sure you do," he cried. "Why, I ain't such a fool, after all. I can see, can't I? I've had my try at it and I've lost, and now you has the better of me. North Inlet? Why, I have no choice, not I! I'll help you sail her, by thunder! So I will."

Well, it seemed to me that there was some sense in this. We made our bargain on the spot. In three minutes I had the *Hispaniola* sailing easily before the wind along the coast of Treasure Island. We had good hopes of reaching the northern point before noon, and coming down again as far as North Inlet before high water.

At high tide we could beach her safely, and wait till low tide to land.

Then I went below to my own chest, where I got a soft silk handkerchief of my mother's. With this, Hands bound up the great cut he had received in the leg. After he had eaten a little and had a swallow or two more of the rum, he began to feel better, and looked almost as well as ever.

We sailed before the breeze like a bird, the coast of the island flashing by, and the view changing every minute. Soon we were past the high lands and beside low, sandy country, and soon we were beyond that again, and had turned the corner of the rocky hill that ends the island on the north.

I was quite happy with my new command, and pleased with the bright, sunny weather and these different views of the coast. I now had plenty of water and good things to eat, and I felt that seizing the *Hispaniola* more than made up for deserting my friends.

Only one thing troubled me—the eyes of Israel Hands seemed to mock me as they followed me about the deck, and an odd smile came and went on his face. It was a smile that had in it both pain and weakness—a dry, old man's smile. But there was something about it that filled me with fear as he watched, and watched, and watched me at my work.

26 *Israel Hands*

The wind, by good luck, now shifted into the west. We could run so much the easier from the northeast corner of the island to the mouth of North Inlet. Only, as we had no power to anchor, and dared not beach her till the tide was high, we had some time to wait. Hands told me how to lay the ship to—that is, to head her directly into the wind and keep her there so that she stood still. After a good many trials I succeeded, and we both sat in silence over another meal.

"Cap'n," said he at last, with that same queer smile, "here's my old shipmate, O'Brien. Suppose you was to toss him overboard. I don't take no blame for killing him, but I don't think he is a pretty sight now, do you?"

"I'm not strong enough and I don't like the job; and there he lies, for all of me," said I.

"This here is an unlucky ship—this *Hispaniola*, Jim," he went on. "There's a lot of men been killed in this ship—a lot of poor seamen dead and gone since you and me took ship in Bristol. I never seen such dirty luck, not I. There was this here O'Brien, now—he's dead, ain't he? Well now, I've never went to school, and you're a lad as can read and figure. Now, do you take it as a dead man is dead for good, or do he come alive again?"

"You can kill the body, Mr. Hands, but not the spirit. You must know that already," I replied. "O'Brien there is in another world, and maybe watching us."

"Ah!" says he. "Well, that's unfortunate—looks as if killing men was a waste of time. However, spirits don't count for much by what I've seen. I'll take a chance with the spirits, Jim. And now, I'll thank you if you'd step down into that there cabin and get me a—well, a—shiver my timbers! I can't hit the name of it. Well, you get me a bottle of wine, Jim—this here rum's too strong for my head."

I could see at once that he had thought up a plan to get rid of me. He wanted me to leave the deck—so much was plain, but I could not imagine why. His eyes never met mine. They kept wandering to and fro, up and down, now with a look to the sky, now with a glance upon the dead O'Brien. All the time he kept smiling and putting his tongue out in the most guilty way, so that a child could have told that he was trying to trick me. I thought that it would be wise to keep the stupid fellow from knowing that I saw through his tricks.

"Some wine?" I said. "Far better. Will you have white or red?"

"Well, I guess it's about the same to me, shipmate," he replied; "just so it's strong, and plenty of it."

"All right," I answered. "I'll bring you red, Mr. Hands. But I'll have to dig for it."

With that I hurried down the stairs with all the noise I could, slipped off my shoes, ran quietly along the gallery, climbed the front ladder, and popped my head out on deck. I knew he would not expect to see me there; yet I took great care not to be seen. And certainly the worst of my fears proved too true.

He was on his hands and knees; and, though his leg seemed to hurt him pretty badly when he moved, yet it was at a good fast rate that he trailed himself across the deck. In half a minute he reached over and picked, out of a pile of rope, a long knife, dark with dried blood. He looked at it for a moment, tried the point upon his hand, and then, hastily hiding it in his coat, hurried back into his old place again.

This was all that I needed to know. Israel could move about; he was now armed. And if he took so much trouble to get rid of me, it was plain that he meant to kill me.

Yet I felt sure that I could trust him in one point, since we both wished the same thing, and that was the saving of the schooner. We both wanted to run her up on the beach, safe enough in a sheltered place, so that, when the time came, she could be got off again with as little trouble as possible. Until that was done I knew that my life would certainly be spared.

While I was thus turning the business over in my mind, I had not been idle. I had stolen back to the cabin, slipped once more into my shoes, seized a bottle of wine, and now, with this in my hand, I came back on deck.

Hands lay as I had left him, all fallen together in a heap and with his eyelids closed, as though he were too weak to bear the light. He looked up, however, at my coming, knocked the neck off the bottle like a man who had done the same thing often, and took a good drink, saying, "Here's luck!" Then he lay quiet for a little, and then, pulling out a stick of tobacco, begged me to cut him a piece.

"Cut me a piece of that," said he, "for I haven't no knife, and hardly strength enough, even if I had. Ah, Jim, Jim, I guess I'm through! Cut me a piece, as will likely be the last, lad. For I'm through, and no mistake."

"Well," said I, "I'll cut you some tobacco. But if I were you and thought myself so badly off, I would say my prayers like a Christian man."

"Why?" said he. "Now, you tell me why."

"Why?" I cried. "You were asking me just now about the dead. You've broken your trust; you've lived in sin and lies and blood; there's a man you killed lying at your feet this moment; and you ask me why! For goodness' sake, Mr. Hands, that's why."

I spoke with a little heat, thinking of the bloody knife he had hidden in his pocket, with which he meant to kill me. He, for his part, took a great drink of the wine.

"For 30 years," he said, "I've sailed the seas, and seen good and bad, fair weather and foul, and what not. Well, now I tell you, I never seen good come of goodness yet. Him that strikes first is best. Dead men don't bite. Them's my views—amen, so be it. And now, you look here," he added, suddenly changing his tone, "the tide's high enough by now. You just take my orders, Cap'n Hawkins, and we'll sail right in and be done with it."

All told, we had about two miles to run; but it was a difficult task to steer the ship into the inlet. The entrance to this northern harbor was not only narrow and shallow, but lay east and west, so that the schooner must be carefully handled to be got in. I obeyed Hands's orders. I am very sure that he was a fine seaman; for we went around and around, and dodged in, just missing the banks.

The shores of North Inlet were as thickly wooded as those of the southern harbor; but the space was long and narrow, and more like the mouth of a river. Right before us, at the southern end, we saw the wreck of a ship in the last stages of decay. It had been a great vessel of three masts, but had lain so long that it was hung about with great strings of seaweed. On the deck, shore bushes had taken root, and now grew thick with flowers. It was a sad sight, but it showed us that the harbor was calm.

"Now," said Hands, "look there. There's a fine spot for to beach a ship in. Fine flat sand, never a breeze, trees all around it, and flowers blooming like a garden on that old ship."

"And once beached," I inquired, "how shall we get her off again?"

"Why, so," he replied. "You take a rope ashore there on the other side at low tide, turn it about one of them big pines; bring it back, turn it around the mast, and wait for the tide. Come high water, all hands take a pull upon the rope, and off she comes as sweet as anything. And now, boy, you stand by. We're near the beach now, and she's going a little too fast. To the right a little—so—steady—right—left a little—steady—steady!"

So he gave his commands, which I obeyed; till, all of a sudden, he cried, "Now, my hearty, into the wind!" And the *Hispaniola* swung round rapidly, and ran head on for the low wooded shore.

I was still so much interested in waiting for the ship to touch shore, that I had quite forgot to keep a watch upon Israel Hands. Instead I stood looking over the side of the ship, watching the ripples spreading wide before the bows. I might have died without a struggle for my life, had not a sudden fear seized me and made me turn my head. Perhaps I had heard a sound, or seen his shadow moving with the tail of my eye. But, sure enough, when I looked round, there was Hands coming toward me, with the knife in his right hand.

We must both have cried aloud when our eyes met. But while mine was the shrill cry of terror, his was a roar of fury. At the same instant he threw himself forward, and I leaped to one side. As I did so, I let go the tiller, which I was still holding to steer the ship. It sprang sharply backward. And I think this saved my life, for it struck Hands across the chest and stopped him, for the moment, in his tracks.

Before he could begin again, I was safe out of the corner where he had me trapped. Just in front of the mainmast, I stopped and drew a pistol from my pocket. I took a cool aim, though he had already turned and was once more coming straight after me, and drew the trigger. There was neither flash nor sound; the powder had been wet with sea water. I cursed myself for my neglect. Why had I not, long before, taken care of my pistols? Then I should not have been running like a helpless sheep before this butcher.

Wounded as he was, it was wonderful how fast he could move, his gray hair tumbling over his face, and his face itself as red as a red flag with his haste and fury. I had no time to try my other pistol and I was sure it would be useless. One thing I saw plainly—I must do more than simply run away from him, or he would soon trap me into the bows, as a moment ago he had so nearly trapped me in the stern. Once so caught, and nine or ten inches of the blood-stained knife would be my last adventure. I placed my palms against the mainmast, which was of a good size, and waited, every nerve stretched.

Seeing that I meant to dodge, he also paused. And a moment or two passed in dodging on his part, and the same movements upon mine. It was a game that I had often played at home on the rocks of Black Hill Cove. But never before, you may be sure, with such a wildly beating heart as now. Still, as I say, it was a boy's game, and I thought I could hold my own at it, against an old seaman with a wounded leg. Indeed, my courage had begun to rise so high that I began to wonder what would be the end of it. While I saw that I could play this game for a long time, I saw no hope of any escape.

Suddenly the *Hispaniola* struck the shore, staggered, and ground for an instant in the sand. Then, swift as a blow, she tipped over to the left side, till the deck stood at an angle of 45 degrees. The sea splashed over and lay in a pool between the deck and the side of the ship.

We were both of us thrown down, and both of us rolled, almost together, over to the side. The dead Red-cap with his arms still spread out, came tumbling stiffly after us. We were so close, indeed, that my head came against Israel's foot with a crack that made my teeth rattle. In spite of the blow, I was the first up again; for Hands had got mixed up with the dead body. The sudden tipping of the ship had made the deck slope so sharply that I could no longer run upon it. I had to find some new way of escape, and that at once, for Israel was almost touching me. Quick as thought, I sprang into the sails, rattled up hand over hand. I did not draw a breath till I was seated on the crosstrees near the top of the mainmast.

I had been saved by being quick. The knife struck not a foot below me, as I was climbing. And there stood Israel Hands with his mouth open and his face turned up to mine, a perfect picture of surprise and disappointment.

Now that I had a moment to myself, I lost no time in loading my pistol, and then, having one ready for use, I now took time to load the second.

Israel began to see the game going against him. After a moment, he also dragged himself heavily into

the sails and, with the knife in his teeth, began slowly to climb. It cost him no end of time and pain to drag his wounded leg behind him. I had quietly finished loading my pistols before he was much more than a third of the way up. Then, with a pistol in either hand, I called him.

"One more step, Mr. Hands," said I, "and I'll blow your brains out! Dead men don't bite, you know," I added with a laugh.

He stopped instantly. I could see by the working of his face that he was trying to think. It took him so long and it was such hard work for him, that I laughed aloud. At last, with a swallow or two, he spoke, his face still wearing the same look of great wonder. In order to speak he had to take the knife from his mouth, but he made no other movement.

"Jim," says he, "I guess we're even, you and me, and we'll have to bargain. I'd have had you except for that there bump, but I don't have no luck, not I. I guess I'll have to give up, which comes hard, you see, for a master seaman like me to a ship's cabin boy like you, Jim."

I was drinking in his words and smiling away, when, suddenly, back went his right hand over his shoulder. Something sang like an arrow through the air. I felt a blow and then a sharp pain, and there I was pinned by the shoulder to the mast. In the horrid pain and surprise of the moment, both my pistols went off, and both fell out of my hands. They did not fall alone. With a choked cry, Israel Hands let go the sails, and plunged head first into the water.

27 *"Pieces of Eight"*

Because the ship was leaning over on its side, the masts hung far out over the water, and from my seat near the top of the mainmast I had nothing below me but the surface of the bay. Hands, who was not so far up, was nearer to the deck and fell between me and the ship. He rose once to the surface, and then sank again for good. As the water settled, I could see him lying in a heap on the clean bright sand in the shadow of the vessel's sides. A fish or two whipped past his body. Sometimes, by the rippling of the water, he seemed to move a little, as if he were trying to rise. But he was dead enough, for all that, being both shot and drowned, and was food for fish in the very place where he had planned my death.

I was no sooner sure of this than I began to feel sick, faint, and terrified. The hot blood was running over my back and chest. The knife, where it had pinned my shoulder to the mast, seemed to burn like a hot iron. Yet it was not so much these real sufferings that frightened me, for it hurt me very little when I used my arm. It was the fear of falling from the mast into that still, green water, beside the body of Israel Hands.

It was my first thought to pull out the knife, but it stuck too hard, and I gave that up with a violent shiver. Oddly enough, that very shiver did the business. The knife, in fact, had almost missed me altogether. It held me by a pinch of skin, and this was torn away by the shiver. Now I was fastened to the mast only by my coat. This I pulled away easily and climbed down to the deck. Then I looked around me, and as the ship was now my own, I began to think of getting rid of its last passenger—the dead man, O'Brien.

He had fallen, as I have said, against the side, where he lay like some horrible, shapeless thing. In that position I could easily lift him over the side. I had now seen so much of death that I had lost almost all my terror for the dead. So I took him by the waist and, with one good swing, tumbled him overboard. He went in with a sounding plunge. The red cap came off, and remained floating on the surface. As soon as the ripple died down, I could see him and Israel lying side by side and the quick fishes swimming to and fro over both.

I was now alone upon the ship. The tide had just turned. The sun would soon set, and already the shadow of the pines began to reach right across the harbor. The evening breeze had sprung up and was singing softly through the ropes of the ship, and the sails began to rattle to and fro.

I began to see a danger to the ship. The smaller jib sails I quickly lowered, and brought tumbling to the deck. But the mainsail was a harder matter. Of course, when the schooner turned over on her side, the mainsail had swung round and down, and a foot or two of the lower end of the sail now hung under water. I thought this made it still more dangerous. Yet the strain was so heavy that I was almost afraid to touch it. At last I got my knife and cut the ropes that fastened the upper end of the big sail to the mast. The peak dropped instantly, and the loose canvas floated out upon the water. Try as I liked, I could not pull the sail down, and that was the best I could do. For the rest, the *Hispaniola* must trust to luck, like myself.

By this time the whole harbor was in shadow—the last rays falling through the woods, and shining bright as jewels on the flowers growing on the old wreck. It began to grow chilly. The tide was rapidly running out, the schooner settling more and more on the sand.

I scrambled forward and looked over. It seemed shallow enough, and holding the cut rope in both hands, I let myself drop softly overboard. The water scarcely reached my waist. The sand was firm and covered with ripple marks. I waded ashore in great spirits, leaving the *Hispaniola* on her side, with her mainsail trailing wide upon the surface of the bay. About the same time the sun went down, and the breeze whistled low among the tossing pines.

At least, and at last, I was off the sea, and I had not returned to shore empty-handed. There lay the schooner, clear at last from pirates and ready for our own men to board and get to sea again. I wished now to get home to the fort and boast of my deeds. Possibly I might be blamed a bit for leaving my friends. But the rescue of the *Hispaniola* was a good answer, and I hoped that even Captain Smollett would say I had not wasted my time.

So thinking, and in fine spirits, I turned my face homeward for the blockhouse and my companions. I remembered that one of the rivers which flow into Captain Kidd's harbor ran from the two-peaked hill upon my left. I turned that way so that I might cross the stream while it was small. The woods were pretty open, and I had soon turned the corner of the hill, and not long after waded across the stream.

This brought me near to where I had first met Ben Gunn; and I walked more carefully, keeping an eye on every side. It was now quite dark, and as I came out from behind the two peaks, I saw a glow against the sky, where, as I thought, Ben Gunn was cooking his supper before a roaring fire. And yet I wondered that he should be so careless. For if I could see this light, might it not reach the eyes of Silver himself where he camped upon the shore among the marshes?

Gradually the night grew blacker. It was all I could do to find my way. The double hill behind me and the Spyglass on my right hand grew fainter and fainter. The stars were few and pale. In the low ground where I wandered I kept tripping among bushes and rolling into sandy pits.

Suddenly a kind of brightness fell about me. I looked up. A pale gleam of moonlight lay on the top of the Spyglass, and soon after I saw something broad and silvery moving low, down behind the trees, and knew the moon was rising.

With this to help me, I made good time; and, sometimes walking, sometimes running, drew near to the fort. Yet, as I began to cross the woods that lie before it, I was careful to walk slowly and watchfully. It would have been a poor end of my adventures to get shot down by my own party by mistake.

The moon was climbing higher and higher; its light began to fall here and there in the more open parts of the woods. And right in front of me a glow of a different color appeared among the trees. It was red and hot, and now and again it was a little darkened—as if it were the coals of a bonfire.

For the life of me, I could not think what it might be.

At last I came right down to the edge of the woods. The western end was already in full moonlight. The rest, and the blockhouse itself, still lay in a black shadow, crossed with long silvery streaks of moonlight. On the other side of the house a huge fire had burned itself into clear coals and shed a steady red light. There was not a soul stirring, nor a sound beside the noises of the breeze.

I stopped, with much wonder in my heart, and perhaps a little terror also. It had not been our way to build great fires. We had, indeed, by the captain's orders, used as little of the wood as possible. I began to fear that something had gone wrong while I was absent.

I stole round by the eastern end, keeping close in shadow, and at a place where the darkness was thickest, crossed the fence.

I got upon my hands and knees and crawled, without a sound, toward the corner of the house. As I drew nearer, my heart grew suddenly light. It is not a pleasant noise that I heard. But just then it was like music to hear my friends snoring together so loud and peaceful in their sleep.

In the meantime, there was no doubt of one thing: they kept a very bad watch. If it had been Silver and his lads that were now creeping in on them, not a soul would have seen daylight. That was what it was, thought I, to have the captain wounded. And again I blamed myself sharply for leaving them in that danger with so few to keep guard.

By this time I had got to the door and stood up. All was dark inside, and I could see nothing. As for sounds, there was the steady snoring of the men, and now and then a slight noise, a very light tapping that I could not understand.

With my arms before me I walked steadily in. I planned to lie down in my own place and enjoy their faces when they found me in the morning.

My foot struck something—it was a sleeper's leg; and he turned and groaned, but without awakening.

And then, all of a sudden, a shrill voice broke forth out of the darkness:

"Pieces of eight! Pieces of eight! Pieces of eight! Pieces of eight! Pieces of eight!" on and on without stopping.

Silver's green parrot, Captain Flint! It was she whom I had heard pecking at a piece of bark. It was she, keeping better watch than any human being, who thus screamed out my presence.

I had no time left me to escape. At the sharp clipping tone of the parrot, the sleepers awoke and sprang up. With a mighty oath, the voice of Silver cried:

"Who goes?"

I turned to run, struck sharply against one person, turned, and ran full into the arms of another, who seized and held me tight.

"Bring a torch, Dick," said Silver.

And one of the men left the log house and soon returned with a lighted torch.

Book **6**

Captain Silver

28 *In the Enemy's Camp*

The red glare of the torch, lighting up the inside of the blockhouse, showed me that the worst of my fears were true. The pirates held the house and stores. There was the barrel of rum, there were the pork and bread, as before; and, to my horror, not a sign of any prisoner. I could only believe that all had died, and my heart grieved me that I had not been there to die with them.

There were six of the pirates, all told. Not another man was left alive. Five of them were on their feet in an instant. The sixth had only risen upon his elbow. He was deadly pale, and the blood-stained cloth round his head told that he had been wounded.

The parrot sat smoothing her feathers, on Long John's shoulder. He himself, I thought, looked somewhat paler and more stern than I was used to. He still wore the fine suit in which he had come to the fort, but it was much the worse for wear, torn and covered with clay.

"So," said he, "here's Jim Hawkins, shiver my timbers! Dropped in, eh? Well, I think that's friendly."

And he sat down upon the rum barrel and began to fill a pipe.

"Give me a light, Dick," said he. Then, when he had a good light, "that'll do, lad," he added. "Stick the torch in the wood pile. You, gentlemen, you needn't stand up for Mr. Hawkins. *He'll* excuse you, you may lay to that. And so, Jim, here you are, and quite a pleasant surprise for poor old John. I see you were smart when first I set my eyes on you, but this here is too much for me to understand."

To all this I made no answer. They had set me with my back against the wall; and I stood there, looking Silver in the face, with black despair in my heart.

Silver took a pull or two at his pipe with great calm, and then went on again.

"Now, you see, Jim, since you *are* here," says he, "I'll give you a piece of my mind. I've always liked you, I have, for a lad of spirit, and the picture of my own self when I was young and handsome. I always wanted you to join me and take your share and die a gentleman. Now, my lad, you've *got* to. Cap'n Smollett's a fine seaman, as I'll own up to any day, but too strict. 'Duty is duty,' says he, and right he is. Just you keep clear of the cap'n, for you ran away from your duty. The doctor himself is gone dead against you—'ungrateful scamp' was what he said. The short and the long of the whole story is this here—you can't go back to your own party, for they won't have you. You'll have to join with Cap'n Silver."

So far so good. My friends, then, were still alive.

"I'm all for talking things over," said Silver. "If you like being with us, well, you'll join. If you don't, Jim, why, you're free to answer no—free and welcome, shipmate. Nothing could be fairer than that, shiver my sides!"

"Am I to answer, then?" I asked, with a trembling voice. Through all this talk, I was made to feel the threat of death that hung over me, and my cheeks burned and my heart beat painfully in my breast.

"Lad," said Silver, "no one's forcing you. Take your time. None of us won't hurry you, mate. Time goes so pleasant in your company, you see."

"Well," says I, growing a bit bolder, "if I'm to choose, I declare I have a right to know what's what, and why you're here, and where my friends are."

"Wot's wot?" repeated one of the pirates with a deep growl. "Ah, he'd be a lucky one as knowed that!"

"You'll perhaps keep quiet till you're spoke to, my friend," cried Silver angrily to this man. And then, in his first sweet tones, he said to me, "Yesterday morning, down came Dr. Livesey with a flag of truce. Says he, 'Cap'n Silver, you're sold out. Ship's gone.' Well, maybe we'd been taking a glass of rum and a song to help it round. I won't say no. Leastways, none of us had looked out. We looked out, and by thunder, the old ship *was* gone. I never seen a bunch of men look so foolish, and you may lay to that. 'Well,' says the doctor, 'let's bargain.' We bargained, him and I, and here we are, stores, rum, blockhouse, and the wood you was thoughtful enough to cut. As for your friends, they've gone. I don't know where they are."

He drew again quietly at his pipe.

"And lest you should take it into that head of yours," he went on, "that you was in the bargain, here's the last word that was said: 'How many are you,' says I, 'to leave?' 'Four,' says the doctor—'four, and one of us wounded. As for that boy, I don't know where he is,' says he, 'nor I don't much care! We're about sick of him.' These was his words."

"Is that all?" I asked.

"Well, it's all that you're to hear, my son," returned Silver.

"And now I am to choose?"

"And now you are to choose, and you may lay to that," said Silver.

"Well," said I, "I'm not such a fool, but I know pretty well what I have to look for. Let the worst come to the worst, it's little I care. I've seen too many die since I fell in with you. But there's a thing or two I have to tell you," I said, and by this time I was quite excited, "and the first is this: here you are, in a bad way; ship lost, treasure lost, men lost; your whole business gone to wreck; and if you want to know who did it—it was I! I was in the apple barrel the night we sighted land. I heard you, John, and you Dick Johnson, and Israel Hands, who is now at the bottom of the sea, and I told every word you said. And as for the schooner, it was I who cut her from her anchor. It was I that killed the men you had aboard of her. It was I who brought her where you'll never see her again, not one of you. The laugh's on my side. I've had the best of it from the first. I no more fear you than I fear a fly. Kill me, if you please, or spare me. But one thing I'll say, and no more. If you spare me, I'll forgive all the things you have done, and when you fellows are in prison for being pirates, I'll save you all I can. It is for you to choose. Kill me and do yourselves no good, or spare me and keep someone to save you from hanging."

I stopped, for, I tell you, I was out of breath. To my wonder, not a man of them moved, but all sat staring at me like as many sheep. And while they were still staring, I broke out again:

"And now, Mr. Silver," I said, "I believe you're the best man here, and if things go to the worst, I'll think it kind of you to let the doctor know the way I took it."

"I'll bear it in mind," said Silver, with a tone so odd that I could not, for the life of me, decide whether he were laughing at me, or was pleased by my courage.

"I'll put one to that," cried the old red-faced seaman—Morgan by name—whom I had seen in Long John's inn in Bristol. "It was him that knowed Black Dog."

"Well, and see here," added Silver. "I'll put another again to that, by thunder! For it was this same boy that stole the chart from Billy Bones. First and last, it's been Jim Hawkins!"

"Then here goes!" said Morgan, with an oath.

And he sprang up, drawing his knife.

"Stop, there!" cried Silver. "Who are you, Tom Morgan? Maybe you thought you was cap'n here, perhaps. By the powers, but I'll teach you better! Cross me, and you'll go where many a good man's gone before you—to feed the fishes. There's never a man crossed me and seen a good day afterward, Tom Morgan, you may lay to that."

Morgan paused, but a low murmur rose from the others.

"Tom's right," said one.

"I stood that kind of talk long enough from one," added another. "I'll be hanged if I'll take it from you, John Silver."

"Did any of you gentlemen want to have it out with *me?*" roared Silver, bending far forward from his place on the barrel, with his pipe still glowing in his right hand. "Him that wants trouble shall get it. You know my way; you're all gentlemen of fortune, by your own word. Well, I'm ready. Take a cutlass, him that dares, and I'll see the color of his inside in spite of my crutch, before that pipe's empty."

Not a man stirred; nor a man answered.

"That's your sort, is it?" he added, putting his pipe back into his mouth. "Well, you're a gay lot to look at, anyway. Not much worth to fight, you ain't. Perhaps you can understand King George's English. I'm cap'n here, by your own choice. I'm cap'n here because I'm the best man by a long way. You won't fight, as gentlemen of fortune should; then, by thunder, you'll obey, and you may lay to it! I like that boy, now. I never seen a better boy than that. He's more a man than any pair of rats of you in this here house, and what I say is this—let me see him that'll lay a hand on him—that's what I say!"

There was a long pause after this. I stood straight up against the wall, my heart still going fast, but with a ray of hope now shining in my bosom. Silver leaned back against the wall, his arms crossed, his pipe in the corner of his mouth, as calm as though he had been in church. But his eye kept wandering, and he kept the tail of it on his followers. They, on their part, drew gradually together toward the far end of the blockhouse, and the low hiss of their whispering sounded in my ear like a stream. One after another, they would look up, and the red light of the torch would fall for a second on their nervous faces. But it was not toward me, it was toward Silver that they turned their eyes.

"You seem to have a lot to say," said Silver, spitting far into the air. "Speak up and let me hear it, or lay to."

"Ax your pardon, sir," returned one of the men, "you're pretty free with some of the rules. Maybe you'll kindly keep an eye upon the rest. This crew's not satisfied. This crew has its rights like other crews. By your own rules, I take it we can talk together. I ax your pardon, sir, as you are the captain right now; but I claim my right and steps outside for a council."

And with a sweeping sea salute, this fellow, a long ill-looking, yellow-eyed man of 35, stepped coolly toward the door and disappeared out of the house. One after another, the rest followed his example; each making a salute as he passed; each adding some excuse. "According to rules," said one. "Seaman's council," said Morgan. And so with one word or another, all marched out and left Silver and me alone with the torch.

Silver instantly removed his pipe.

"Now, look you here, Jim Hawkins," he said, in a steady whisper. "You're within half an inch of death, and, what's a long sight worse, of torture. They're going to vote me out as captain. But I'll stand by you through thick and thin. I didn't mean to. No, not till you spoke up. I was in a bad frame of mind about losing that treasure and getting hanged into the bargain. But I see you was the right sort. I says to myself, You stand by Hawkins and Hawkins'll stand by you. I'm your last card, Jim, and, by the living thunder, you're *my* last card! Back to back, says I. I'll save you as my witness, and you'll save my neck!"

I began to understand.

"You mean all's lost?" I asked.

"Ay, by gum, I do!" he answered. "Ship gone, neck gone—that's the size of it. When I looked into that bay, Jim Hawkins, and seen no schooner—well, I'm tough, but I gave out. As for that crew and their council, mind you, they're just fools and cowards. I'll save your life—if I can—from them. But see here, Jim, you reward me by saving me from hanging when we gets back to England."

I was confused. It seemed a thing so hopeless he was asking—he, the old pirate, the leader from the first.

"What I can do, that I'll do," I said.

"It's a bargain!" cried Long John. "You speak well of me, and, by thunder, I've a chance."

He hobbled to the torch, where it had been set in the wood pile, and took a fresh light for his pipe.

"Understand me, Jim," he said, returning. "I've a good head on my shoulders, I have. I'm on squire's side now. I know you've got that ship safe somewheres. How you done it, I don't know, but safe it is. I guess Hands and O'Brien must have gone over to your side. I never much believed in neither of *them*. I'll ask you no question, nor I won't let others. I know when a game's up, I do; and I know a lad that's brave."

He drew some rum from the barrel into a can.

"Will you taste, shipmate?" he asked. And when I had refused, "Well, I'll take a drink myself, Jim," said he. "I need strength, for there's trouble on hand. And talking of trouble, why did that doctor give me the chart, Jim?"

The wonder in my face told him I knew nothing about it.

"Ah, well, he did, though," said he. "And there's something queer about that—something queer, surely, about that, Jim—bad or good."

And he took another swallow of the rum, shaking his great fair head like a man who looks forward to the worst.

29 The Black Spot Again

The council of the pirates had lasted some time, when one of them came into the blockhouse, and with the same salute, asked for the torch. Silver agreed; and the man went out again, leaving us together in the dark.

"There's a fight coming, Jim," said Silver, who had, by this time, taken on quite a friendly and familiar tone.

I turned to the opening nearest me and looked out. The coals of the great fire had so far burned themselves out, and there was so little light from it, that I understood why the pirates wanted a torch. About halfway down the slope to the fort, they were gathered in a group. One held the light. Another was on his knees in their midst, and I saw the blade of an open knife shine in his hand. The rest were all somewhat stooping, as though watching this man. I could just make out that he had a book as well as a knife in his hand. The kneeling figure rose once more to his feet, and the whole party began to move together toward the house.

"Here they come," said I. And I returned to my place at the wall, for I did not want them to find me watching them.

"Well, let them come, lad—let them come," said Silver cheerfully. "I've still another card to play."

The door opened, and the five men, standing close together just inside pushed one of their number forward. At any other time it would have been funny to see how slowly he came forward, holding his closed right hand in front of him.

"Step up, lad," cried Silver. "I won't eat you. Hand it over, fool. I know the rules, I do. I won't hurt you."

The pirate stepped forward more quickly, passed something to Silver, from hand to hand, and slipped yet more quickly back again to his companions.

Silver looked at what had been given him.

"The black spot! I thought so," he said. "Where might you have got the paper? Why, hello! Look here, now; this ain't lucky. You've gone and cut this out of a Bible. What fool cut a Bible?"

"Ah, there!" said Morgan—"There! Wot did I say? No good'll come of that, I said."

"Well, you've about fixed it now, among you," continued Silver. "You'll all hang now, I guess. What soft-headed fool had a Bible?"

"It was Dick," said one.

"Dick, was it? Then Dick can get to his prayers," said Silver. "He's seen the last of his luck, has Dick, and you may lay to that."

But here the long man with the yellow eyes struck in.

"Stop that talk, John Silver," he said. "This crew has tipped you the black spot, as in duty bound. Just you turn it over, as in duty bound, and see what's wrote there. Then you can talk."

"Thank you, George," replied Silver. "You always had the rules by heart, George, as I'm pleased to see. Well, what is it, anyway? Ah! 'Voted out'—that's it, is it? Very pretty wrote, to be sure. Like print, I declare. Your writing, George? Why, you are getting to be quite a leading man in this here crew. You'll be cap'n next, I shouldn't wonder. Just oblige me with that torch again, will you? This pipe don't draw."

"Come, now," said George, "you don't fool this crew no more. You're not our captain any more, and you'll maybe step down off that barrel, and help vote for the next captain."

"I thought you said you knowed the rules," returned Silver. "Anyway, if you don't, I do. And I wait here—and I'm still your cap'n, mind you—till you say what you have to complain about, and I answer. In the meantime, your black spot ain't worth a cent. After that, we'll see."

"Oh," replied George, "you don't need to be afraid. We all agree, we do. First, you've made a failure of this cruise—you'll be a bold man to say no to that. Second, you let the enemy out of this here trap for nothing. Why did they want out? I dunno; but it's pretty plain they wanted it. Third, you wouldn't let us attack them when they were leaving. Oh, we see through you, John Silver. You want to play double; that's what's wrong with you. And then, fourth, there's this here boy."

"Is that all?" asked Silver quietly.

"Enough, too," replied George. "We'll all hang for your mistakes."

"Well, now, look here, I'll answer these four points; one after another I'll answer 'em. I made a failure of this cruise, did I? Well, now you all know what *I* wanted. And you all know, if that had been done, we'd have been aboard the *Hispaniola* this very night, every man of us alive and fit and full of good plum pudding, and the treasure in the ship, by thunder! Well, who crossed me? Who forced my hand, me that had the right to be captain? Who tipped me the black spot the day we landed, and began this trouble? Who done it? Why, it was Anderson and Hands and you, George Merry! And you're the last alive of the three of you. And you dare to want to be captain over me—you, that sank the lot of us! By the powers!"

Silver paused, and I could see by the faces of George and his comrades that his words had a powerful effect.

"That's for number one," cried Silver, wiping his brow, for he had been talking with such force that he shook the house. "Why, I give you my word, I'm foolish to speak to you. You've neither sense nor memory, and I wonder where your mother was that let you come to sea. Sea! Gentlemen of fortune! *Pirates!* I say you'd make better tailors than pirates!"

"Go on, John," said Morgan. "We complained of other things too."

"Ah, the others!" returned John. "They're a nice lot, ain't they? You say this cruise is ruined. Ah! if you could understand how bad it's ruined, you would see! We're that near the hangman that my neck's stiff with thinking on it. You've seen pirates, maybe, hanged in chains, birds flying round them, and seamen pointing them out as they go past? And you've heard their chains rattle as they swing? Now, that's about where we are, every one of us, thanks to him and Hands and Anderson, and other fools of you.

"And if you want to know about that boy, why, shiver my timbers! Isn't he one of their party, and won't they want him back? And if he is our prisoner, we can bargain with them, can't we? Are we a-going to waste a chance like that? No, not us! He might be our last chance, too! Kill that boy? Not me, mates.

"And another thing! Maybe you don't think it a good thing to have a real college doctor come to see you every day—you, John, with your head broke open—or you, George Merry, that had the fever shakes on you not six hours ago, and your eyes the color of lemon peel to this minute. And maybe you don't know there was a sister ship of the *Hispaniola* coming, either? But there is; and not so long till then; and we'll see who'll be glad to have a prisoner when it comes to that. And as for the last, and why I made a bargain—well, you came crawling on your knees to me to make it—on your knees you came, you was that gloomy—and you'd have starved, too, if I hadn't—for all our food was on the schooner. But that's nothing! You look there— *that's* why!"

And he threw down upon the floor a paper that I knew at once. It was the chart on yellow paper, with the three red crosses, that I had found at the bottom of Billy Bones's chest. Why the doctor had given it to him was more than I could understand.

But if it were a puzzle to me, the sight of the chart was more than the pirates could believe. They leaped upon it like cats upon a mouse. It went from hand to hand, one tearing it from another. By the oaths and the cries and the laughter with which they studied it, you would have thought that they had the gold and were at sea with it in safety.

"Yes," said one, "that's Flint, sure enough. *J. F.*, and a mark below; so he done always."

"Mighty pretty," said George. "But how are we to get away with it, and us no ship?"

Silver suddenly sprang up and leaned against the wall. "Now I give you warning, George," he cried. "One more word from you, and I'll call you down and fight you. How are we going to get the gold away? Why, how do I know? *You* had ought to tell me that—you and the rest, that lost me my schooner. But not you, you can't; you haven't got the brains of a fly. But you can speak polite, and shall, too, George Merry, you may lay to that."

"That's fair enough," said old man Morgan.

"Fair! I guess so," said Silver. "You lost the ship; I found the treasure. Who's the better man at that? And now I'm through, by thunder! Elect whom you please to be your captain now. I'm done with it."

"Silver!" they cried. "Silver forever! Silver for cap'n!"

"So that's the tune, is it?" cried John. "George, I reckon you'll have to wait again to be cap'n, friend. And lucky for you that I'm not a mean man. But that was never my way. And now shipmates, this black spot? It ain't much good now, is it? Dick's broke his luck and spoiled his Bible, and that's about all."

Dick was unhappy at the curse he had brought upon himself.

"A Bible with a bit cut out!" said Silver. "It's no better than a song book now."

"Ain't it, though?" cried Dick. "Well, I guess a song book is worth having, too."

"Here, Jim—here's something for you," said Silver. And he tossed me the paper.

It was a round piece of a page cut from the Bible. One side was blank, for it had been the last leaf. The other contained a verse or two of Revelation—these words among the rest, which struck sharply home upon my mind: "Without are dogs and murderers." The printed side had been blackened with a piece of burnt wood from the fire. On the blank side had been written with the same material the words, "Voted out."

That was the end of the night's business. Soon after, with a drink all round, we lay down to sleep; and to punish George Merry, Silver made him a guard for the night.

It was long before I could close an eye, and Heaven knows I had plenty to think about: the man whom I had killed that afternoon; my own great danger; and, above all, the clever game that I saw Silver now playing—keeping the mutineers together with one hand, and reaching with the other after every possible thing that might save his miserable life. He himself slept peacefully and snored aloud. Yet my heart was sore for him, wicked as he was, to think on the dark danger he faced, and the shameful hanging that would probably be his end.

30 _A Pledge of Honor_

I was wakened by a clear, hearty voice calling from the edge of the wood.

"Blockhouse, ahoy!" it cried. "Here's the doctor."

And the doctor it was. He must have got up in the dark, for it was scarcely day. When I ran to an opening and looked out, I saw him standing, like Silver once before, up to the middle of the leg in creeping fog.

"You, doctor! Top of the morning to you, sir!" cried Silver, broad awake and beaming with good nature in a moment. "Bright and early, to be sure; and it's the early bird that gets the worm. George, hurry up, son, and help Dr. Livesey over the fence. All a-doin' well, your patients was—all well and merry."

So he chattered on, standing on the hilltop, with his crutch under his elbow and one hand upon the side of the log house—quite the same old John in voice, manner, and word.

"We've quite a surprise for you, too, sir," he went on. "We've a little stranger here—he! He! A new boarder and roomer, sir, and looking fit as a fiddle. Slept, he did, right alongside of John—side by side we was, all night."

Dr. Livesey was by this time across the fence and pretty near Silver. I could hear the change in his voice as he said:

"Not Jim?"

"The very same Jim as ever was," says Silver.

The doctor stopped short, although he did not

speak, and it was some seconds before he seemed able to move on.

"Well, well," he said at last, "duty first and pleasure afterward, as you might have said yourself, Silver. Let us look at these patients of yours."

A moment afterward he had entered the blockhouse, and, with one grim nod to me, went on with his work among the sick. He did not seem to be afraid, though he must have known that his life, among these evil men, was in constant danger. He rattled on to his patients as if he were paying a visit in a quiet English family. The men treated him as if nothing had happened—as if he were still ship's doctor, and they still faithful hands before the mast.

"You're doing well, my friend," he said to the fellow with the wounded head, "and if ever any person had a close shave, it was you. Your head must be as hard as iron. Well, George, how goes it? You're a pretty color, certainly. Why, you must have a fever, man. Did you take that medicine? Did he take that medicine, men?"

"Ay, ay, sir, he took it, sure enough," returned Morgan.

"Because, you see, since I am mutineers' doctor, or prison doctor, as I prefer to call it," says Dr. Livesey in his pleasantest way, "I make it a point of honor not to lose a man for King George (God bless him!) and the hangman."

The rascals looked at each other, but said nothing.

"Dick don't feel well, sir," said one.

"Don't he?" replied the doctor. "Well, step up here, Dick, and let me see your tongue. Well, I'm not surprised! The man's tongue is fit to frighten the French. Another fever."

"Ah, there," said Morgan, "That comed of tearing Bibles."

"That comed—as you call it—of being silly fools," cried the doctor, "and not having sense enough to know pure air from poison, and the dry land from a swamp. I think it most likely that you'll all have a fever sooner or later. Camp in a swamp, will you? Silver, I'm surprised at you. You're less of a fool than many, take you all around; but you don't appear to me to have the least idea of the rules of health."

"Well," he added, after he had looked them all over, and they had taken his medicines, more like good schoolchildren than blood-guilty pirates—"well, that's done for today. And now I should wish to have a talk with that boy, please."

And he nodded his head toward me.

George Merry was at the door, and he swung round and cried "No!" and swore.

Silver struck the barrel with his open hand.

"Silence!" he roared, and looked about him exactly like a lion. "Doctor," he went on, in his usual tones, "I was a-thinking of that, knowing how you liked the boy. We're all grateful for your kindness, and, as you see, the crew puts faith in you, and takes the drugs down like that much rum. And I take it I've found a way that will suit all. Hawkins, will you give me your word of honor as a young gentleman—for a young gentleman you are—your word of honor not to run away?"

I gave the promise.

"Then, doctor," said Silver, "you just step outside of that fence, and when you're there, I'll bring the boy down on the inside, and I guess you can talk through the fence. Good day to you, sir, and all our duties to the squire and Cap'n Smollett."

The roar of anger, which nothing but Silver's black looks had kept back, broke out as soon as the doctor had left the house. Silver was told that he was playing double—that he was trying to make a separate peace for himself—that he was selling out his friends. Of course, that is exactly what he was doing. It seemed so clear to me, in this case, that I could not imagine how he was to face their anger. But he was twice the man the rest were. He called them all fools, said it was necessary I should talk to the doctor, fluttered the chart in their faces, and asked them if they could afford to break the bargain the very day they were going treasure hunting.

"No, by thunder!" he cried, "it's us must break the bargain when the time comes. And till then I'll fool that doctor, if I have to oil his boots with rum."

And then he told them to get the fire lit and stalked out upon his crutch, with his hand on my shoulder, leaving them silent.

"Slow, lad, slow," he said. "They might fall upon us in a twinkle of an eye, if we was seen to hurry."

Very slowly, then, did we walk across the sand to where the doctor waited for us on the other side of the fence, and as soon as we were within easy speaking distance, Silver stopped.

"You'll make a note of this here also, doctor," says he, "and the boy will tell you how I saved his life, and was voted out for it, too, and you may lay to that. Doctor, when a man's taking as many chances as me, you wouldn't think it too much to give him one good word? You'll please bear in mind it's not my life only now—it's that boy's into the bargain. And you'll speak well of me, doctor, and give me a bit of hope to go on, for the sake of mercy?"

Silver was a changed man, now that he was out there and had his back to his friends and the block-house. His cheeks seemed to have fallen in; his voice trembled. Never was a man more dead in earnest.

"Why, John, you're not afraid?" asked Dr. Livesey.

"Doctor, I'm no coward; no, not I—not *so* much!" and he snapped his fingers. "If I was, I wouldn't say this. But I'll own up, I've the fear of hanging upon me. You're a good man and true. I never seen a better man! And you'll not forget what I done that was good, not any more than you'll forget the bad, I know. And I step aside—see here—and leave you and Jim alone. And you'll remember that too, at the right time, won't you?"

So saying, he stepped back a little way till he was out of hearing, and there sat down upon a tree stump and began to whistle. Now and again he would spin round upon his seat so as to be able to see, sometimes me and the doctor, and sometimes his followers, as they went to and fro in the sand between the fire and the house, making breakfast.

"So, Jim," said the doctor, sadly, "here you are. As you have sown, so shall you reap, my boy. Heaven knows, I cannot find it in my heart to blame you. But this much I will say: when Captain Smollett was well, you dared not have gone off; and when he was ill, and couldn't help it, by George, it was really cowardly!"

I began to weep. "Doctor," I said, "you might spare me. I have blamed myself enough. My life's in danger, and I should have been dead by now, if Silver hadn't saved me. Doctor, believe this, I can die—and I suppose I deserve it—but what I fear is torture. If they come to torture me—"

"Jim," the doctor broke in, and his voice was quite

changed, "Jim, I can't have this. Whip over, and we'll run for it."

"Doctor," said I, "I gave my word."

"I know, I know," he cried. "We can't help that now, Jim. I'll take the blame, my boy; but I cannot let you stay here. Jump! One jump, and you're out, and we'll run for it like deer."

"No," I replied, "you know right well you wouldn't do the thing yourself, neither you, nor squire, nor captain. And neither will I. Silver trusted me. I gave my word, and back I go. But, doctor, you did not let me finish. If they come to torture me, I might let slip a word of where the ship is. For I got the ship, part by luck and part by risking, and she lies in North Inlet on the southern beach, and just below high water. At half tide she must be high and dry."

"The ship!" exclaimed the doctor.

Quickly I told him my story, and he heard me out in silence.

"There is a kind of fate in this," he said when I had finished. "Every step, it's you that saves our lives. And do you suppose by any chance that we are going to let you lose yours? That would be a poor return, my boy. You found out the plot; you found Ben Gunn—the best deed that ever you did, or will do, though you live to be 90. Silver," he cried, "Silver—I'll give you a piece of advice," he went on, as John drew near again, "don't you be in any great hurry after that treasure."

"Why, sir, I do my best, and waiting ain't good," said Silver. "I can only save my life and the boy's by looking for that treasure. You may lay to that."

"Well, Silver," replied the doctor, "if that is so, I'll

go one step further. Look out for trouble when you find it."

"Sir," said Silver, "as between man and man, that's saying too much and too little. What you're after, why you left the blockhouse, why you've given me that there chart, I don't know now, do I? Yet I done what you told me with my eyes shut and never a word of hope! But no, this here's too much. Tell me what you mean plain out."

"No," said the doctor, "I've no right to say more. It's not my secret, you see, Silver, or I'd tell it to you. But I'll go as far with you as I dare go, and a step further. First, I'll give you a bit of hope. Silver, if we both get out of this wolf-trap alive, I'll do my best to save you."

Silver's face was shining. "You couldn't say more, I'm sure, sir, not if you was my mother," he cried.

"Well, that's my first promise," added the doctor. "My second is a piece of advice. Keep the boy close beside you, and when you need help, shout. I'm off to seek it for you, and that itself will show you that I mean what I say. Good-bye, Jim."

And Dr. Livesey shook hands with me through the fence, nodded to Silver, and set off at a rapid pace into the wood.

31 The Treasure Hunt — Flint's Pointer

"Jim," said Silver, when we were alone, "if I saved your life, you saved mine; and I'll not forget it. I seen the doctor waving you to run for it—with the tail of my eye, I did; and I seen you say no, as plain as hearing. Jim that's one for you. This is the first hope I had since the attack failed, and I owe it to you. And now, Jim, we're to go in for this here treasure hunting without knowing much about it, and I don't like it. You and me must stick close, back to back like, and we'll save our necks in spite of everything."

Just then a man called to us from the fire that breakfast was ready, and we were soon seated here and there about the sand with our bread and pork. They had lit a fire fit to roast an ox, and it had now grown so hot that they could scarcely go near it. They had cooked three times more than we could eat. One of them, with an empty laugh, threw what was left into the fire, which blazed and roared again. I never in my life saw men so careless of the future. Hand to mouth is the only word that fit their way of doing. What with wasted food and sleeping guards, I could see that they would not be able to carry on a long struggle.

Even Silver, eating away with Captain Flint upon his shoulder, had not a word of blame for them. And this surprised me, for I thought he had never shown himself so cunning as he did then.

"Ay, mates," said he, "it's lucky you have old Silver to think for you with this here head. I got what I wanted, I did. Sure enough, they have the ship. Where they have it, I don't know yet. But once we find the treasure, we'll have to jump around and find out. And then, mates, us that has the boats, I guess, has the upper hand."

Thus he kept running on, with his mouth full of the hot pork. Thus he kept up their hopes and their faith in him.

"As for our prisoner, Jim here," he went on, "that's his last talk, I guess, with them he loves so dear. I've got my piece of news, and thanks to him for that. I'll take him on a rope when we go treasure hunting, for we'll keep him like so much gold, in case anything goes wrong. Once we get the ship and treasure both, and are off to sea like jolly companions, why, then we'll toss Mr. Hawkins over, we will. And we'll give him his share, to be sure, for all his kindness."

It was no wonder the men were in a good humor now. For my part, I was horribly gloomy. I knew exactly what Silver meant by my "share" and I knew I would not be spared. I had no doubt that he would try his best to carry out this plan he was making with the pirates. If successful, he would have wealth and freedom with the pirates. On the other hand, if the plan failed, he could fall back on the doctor's promise to help him escape hanging. Thus he played a double game.

If things turned out in such a way that he was forced to keep his word to Dr. Livesey, even then what danger lay before us! Suppose his followers found out that he had played a double game, and he and I should have to fight for dear life—he, a cripple, and I, a boy—against five strong and active seamen!

Besides, I could not understand why my friends had left the fort; why they had given the chart to Silver; and what the doctor had meant when he said to Silver, "Look out for trouble when you find it." I had very little taste for my breakfast, and with a heavy heart I set out behind the pirates on the treasure hunt.

We were a strange sight—all in soiled sailor clothes, and all except me armed to the teeth. Silver had two guns hung about him—one before and one behind—besides the great cutlass at his waist and a pistol in each pocket of his coat. Captain Flint sat perched upon his shoulder, chattering away at odds and ends of sea talk. I had a rope about my waist and followed after Silver, who held the loose end, now in his free hand, now between his powerful teeth. For all the world, I was led like a dancing bear.

Some of the men carried picks and shovels—for that had been the very first thing they brought ashore from the *Hispaniola*. Others carried pork, bread, and rum for the noon meal. All the food came from our stock, and I could see the truth of Silver's words the night before. If he had not struck a bargain with the doctor, he and his men would have had to live on what they could kill by hunting, and drink water from the streams of the island. All their food, of course, had been left on the *Hispaniola*. Water would have been little to their taste; a sailor is not usually a good shot. And, besides all that, it was not likely they had much powder and shot.

Well, we all set out—even the fellow with the broken head, who should have kept in the shade—and trailed, one after another, to the beach, where the two gigs were lying.

As we pulled across the harbor, there was some talk about the chart. The red cross was, of course, far too large to be a guide. And the directions on the back of the note were not clear. They ran, the reader may remember, thus:

> "Tall tree, Spyglass Shoulder, bearing a point to the N. of N.N.E.
> "Skeleton Island E.S.E. and by E.
> "Ten feet."

A tall tree was thus the chief mark. The shore right before us was 200 or 300 feet high, sloping on the north up to the high hill called the Spyglass, and on the south to the other hill, the Mizzenmast. The top of this high cliff was dotted thickly with pine trees. Every here and there, one of these trees rose 40 or 50 feet above the others. One of these must be the "tall tree" of Capt. Flint's map, but which one could only be found out by taking the readings from the compass on the spot.

Every man in the boats had picked a favorite tree of his own before we were halfway over. Long John alone shrugged his shoulders and told them to wait till they were there.

We pulled easily, by Silver's orders, so as not to tire the men, and, after quite a long passage, landed at the mouth of the second river—the one which runs down from the Spyglass. From this place, turning left, we began to climb the slope toward the top of the cliff.

Little by little the hill began to get steeper and become stony under foot. The woods grew more open here. It was a pleasant part of the island that we were now nearing. Fragrant bushes and many flowering plants had almost taken the place of grass. Thickets of green trees were dotted here and there with the red trunks and the broad shadow of the pines. The air was fresh and wonderfully cool.

The party spread out in a fan shape, shouting and leaping to and fro. About the center, and a good way behind the rest, Silver and I followed—I tied by my rope, he plowing along and breathing hard, among the sliding gravel. From time to time, indeed, I had to lend him a hand, or he would have missed his step and fallen backward down the hill.

We had climbed for about half a mile and were nearing the top of the cliff, when the man on the left began to cry aloud, as if in terror. Shout after shout came from him, and the others began to run toward him.

"He can't have found the treasure," said old Morgan, hurrying past us from the right, "for that's away up on top."

We found that it was something very different. At the foot of a pretty big pine, a human skeleton lay, with a few pieces of clothing, on the ground. I believe a chill struck for a moment to every heart.

"He was a seaman," said George Merry, who, bolder than the rest, had gone up close and was studying the rags of clothing. "Anyways, this is good sea cloth."

"Ay, ay," said Silver, "likely enough. But what kind of a way is that for bones to lie? It ain't natural."

The man lay perfectly straight—his feet pointing in one direction, his hands, raised above his head, pointing directly in the other.

"I've taken a notion into my old head," said Silver. "Here's the compass. There's the tiptop point of Skeleton Island, sticking out like a tooth. Just read the compass, will you, along the line of them bones."

It was done. The body pointed straight in the direction of the island, and the compass read *E.S.E. and by E.*

"I thought so," cried Silver. "This here is a pointer. Right up there is our line for the treasure. But, by thunder, if it don't make me cold inside to think of Flint. This is one of *his* jokes, and no mistake. Him and these six men was alone here; he killed them, every man. And this one he dragged here and laid by compass, shiver my timbers! They're long bones, and the hair's been yellow. Yes, that would be Allardyce. You remember Allardyce, Tom Morgan?"

"Ay, ay," returned Morgan, "I remember him. He owed me money, he did, and took my knife ashore with him."

"Speaking of knives," said another, "why don't we find his lying round? Flint wasn't the man to pick a seaman's pocket."

"By the powers, and that's true!" cried Silver.

"There ain't a thing left here," said Merry, still feeling round among the bones, "not a copper nor a tobaccy box. It don't look natural to me."

"No, by gum, it don't," agreed Silver; "not natural, nor not nice, says you. Great guns, mates, if Flint was living, this would be a hot spot for you and me. Six they were, and six are we. And bones is what they are now."

"I saw Flint dead with these here eyes," said Morgan. "Billy Bones took me in. There he laid, with pennies on his eyes."

"Dead—ay, sure enough he's dead and gone below," said the fellow with the wounded head; "but if ever a spirit walked, it would be Flint's. Dear heart, but he died bad, did Flint!"

"Ay, that he did," said another. "Now he raged, and now he yelled for rum, and now he sang. 'Fifteen Men' were his only song, mates; and I tell you true, I never rightly liked to hear it since. It was very hot and the window was open, and I could hear that old song coming out as clear as clear."

"Come, come," said Silver, "stop this talk. He's dead, and he don't walk, that I know. Anyways, he won't walk in daylight, and you may lay to that. March ahead for the treasure."

We started, certainly. But in spite of the hot sun and the bright daylight, the pirates no longer ran separate and shouting through the wood, but kept side by side and spoke softly. The terror of the dead pirate had fallen on their spirits.

32 The Treasure Hunt—The Voice Among the Trees

Partly because their spirits were low after their scare, partly to rest Silver and the sick folk, the whole party sat down as soon as they had reached the top of the cliff.

The land sloped a little toward the west. From this spot, we could see a long way in either direction. Before us, over the treetops, we saw the Cape of the Woods. Behind we not only looked down upon the harbor and Skeleton Island, but saw—clear across the sand point—a great field of open sea to the east. Above us rose the Spyglass, here dotted with single pines, there black with great rocks. There was no sound but that of the distant sea and the hum of insects in the brush.

Silver, as he sat, took readings from his compass.

"There are three 'tall trees,'" said he, "about in the right line from Skeleton Island. 'Spyglass Shoulder,' I take it, means that lower point there. It's child's play to find the stuff now. I've half a mind to eat first."

"I don't feel well," growled Morgan. "Thinking of Flint—I think it were—as done me."

"Ah, well, my son, you can thank your stars he's dead," said Silver.

"He were an ugly devil," cried a third pirate, with a shiver. "Blue in the face, too!"

"That was how the rum took him," added Merry. "Blue! Well, I reckon he was blue. That's a true word."

Ever since they had found the skeleton, they had spoken lower and lower. They had almost got to whispering by now, so that the sound of their talk hardly broke the silence of the wood. All of a sudden, out of the middle of the trees in front of us, a thin, high, trembling voice struck up the well-known air and words:

> "Fifteen men on the dead man's chest—
> Yo-ho-ho, and a bottle of rum!"

I never have seen men more dreadfully scared than the pirates. The color went from their six faces like magic. Some leaped to their feet; some took hold of others; Morgan fell to the ground.

"It's Flint, by—!" cried Merry.

The song had stopped as suddenly as it began— broken off, you would have said, in the middle of a note. As though someone had laid his hand upon the singer's mouth.

"Come," said Silver, struggling with white lips to get the word out, "this won't do. Stand by to go about. This is a poor start, and I can't name the voice. But it's someone tricking us—someone that's flesh and blood, and you may lay to that."

His courage had come back as he spoke, and some of the color to his face along with it. Already the others had begun to listen to him and were gaining courage, when the same voice broke out again—not singing this time, but in a faint distant hail.

"Darby M'Graw," it cried, "Darby M'Graw! Darby M'Graw!" again and again and again. Then rising a little higher, and with an oath that I leave out, "Fetch back the rum, Darby!"

The pirates remained rooted to the ground, their eyes starting from their heads. Long after the voice had died away they still stared in silence, fearfully, before them.

"That fixes it!" gasped one. "Let's go!"

"They was his last words," moaned Morgan, "Flint's last words before he died."

Dick had his Bible out and was praying. He had been well brought up, had Dick, before he came to sea and fell among bad companions.

Still, Silver was not beaten. I could hear his teeth rattle in his head, but he had not yet given up.

"Nobody in this here island ever heard of Darby," he muttered, "not one but us that's here." And then, making a great effort, "Shipmates," he cried, "I'm here to get that treasure, and I'll not be beat by man nor devil. I never was feared of Flint in his life and, by the powers, I'll face him dead. There's 700,000 pounds not a quarter of a mile from here. When did ever a gentleman of fortune turn his back on that much money for a drunken old seaman with a blue mug—and him dead, too?"

But there was no sign of courage in his followers. Indeed, they seemed more frightened than ever by his words.

"Stop that, John!" said Merry. "Don't you cross a spirit."

And the rest were all too terrified to reply. They would have run away had they dared. But fear kept them together and kept them close by John, as if his daring helped them. He, on his part, had pretty well fought his fear down.

"Spirit? Well, maybe," he said. "But there's one thing not clear to me. There was an echo. Now, no man ever seen a spirit with a shadow; well, then, what's he doing with an echo to him, I should like to know? That ain't in nature, surely?"

"Well, that's so," George said. "You've a head upon your shoulders, John, and no mistake. And come to think of it, it was like Flint's voice, all right, but not just exactly like it, after all. It was more like somebody else's voice now—it was more like—"

"By the powers, Ben Gunn!" roared Silver.

"Ay, and so it were," cried Morgan, springing on his knees. "Ben Gunn it were!"

"It don't make much difference, do it?" asked Dick. "Ben Gunn's not here in the body, any more than Flint."

"Why nobody minds Ben Gunn," cried Merry. "Dead or alive, nobody minds him."

It was surprising how their good spirits returned, and how the color came back into their faces. Soon they were talking together, stopping now and then to listen. Not long after, hearing no further sound, they gathered their tools and set forth again. Merry walked first with Silver's compass to keep them on the right line with Skeleton Island. He had said the truth; dead or alive, nobody minded Ben Gunn.

Dick alone still held his Bible and looked around him as he went, with fearful glances. But he found no sympathy, and Silver even teased him for it.

"I told you," said he—"I told you, you had spoiled your Bible. If it ain't no good any more, what do you suppose a spirit would care for it? Not that!" and he snapped his big fingers, halting a moment on his crutch.

But Dick was still unhappy; indeed, it was soon plain to me that the lad was sick. The fever which Dr. Livesey had warned them about, was upon him.

It was fine open walking here. Our way lay a little downhill, for, as I have said, the land sloped toward the west. The pines, great and small, grew wide apart, and wide open spaces baked in the hot sunshine.

The first of the tall trees was reached, and by the reading, proved to be the wrong one. So with the second. The third rose nearly 200 feet into the air above a clump of bushes, a giant of a tree, with a red trunk as big as a cottage. It could be seen far to sea both on the east and west, and might have been used as a sailing mark upon the map.

But it was not its size that now interested my companions. It was the knowledge that 700,000 pounds in gold lay somewhere buried below its spreading shadow. The thought of the money, as they drew nearer, swallowed up their fears. Their eyes burned in their heads; their feet grew faster and lighter. Their whole soul was bound up in that fortune, that whole lifetime of ease and pleasure that lay waiting there for each of them.

Silver hobbled on his crutch, breathing hard. His nostrils stood out and quivered. He cursed when the flies settled on his hot and shiny face. He jerked at the rope that held me to him, and, from time to time, turned his eyes upon me with a deadly look. Certainly he took no pains to hide his thoughts; and certainly I read them like print. Because of the nearness of the gold, everything else had been forgotten. His promise and the doctor's warning were both things of the past. I knew that he hoped to seize upon the treasure, find and board the *Hispaniola* during the night, cut every honest person's throat on that island, and sail away as he had at first meant to, loaded with crimes and riches.

Shaken as I was with these fears, it was hard for me to keep up with the rapid pace of the treasure hunters. Now and again I stumbled. It was then that Silver pulled so roughly at the rope and threw at me his deadly glances. Dick, who had dropped behind us and now brought up the rear, was muttering to himself both prayers and curses as his fever kept rising. This also added to my misery. To make it even worse, I kept thinking of Captain Flint and his blue face. How he had died singing and shouting for drink; how he had, right here on this island, killed with his own hand, his six followers.

We were now at the edge of the woods.

"Hurrah, mates, all together!" shouted Merry. And they broke into a run.

And suddenly, not ten yards further, we saw them stop. A low cry arose. Silver doubled his pace, digging away with the foot of his crutch like a wild man. Next moment he and I had come also to a dead halt.

Before us was a great hole, made some time ago, for the sides had fallen in and grass was growing on the bottom. In this were the handle of a pick broken in two and the boards of several packing cases lying around. On one of these boards I saw, burned on with a hot iron, the name *Walrus* — the name of Flint's ship.

All was clear to everyone. The hiding place of the treasure had been found and robbed. The 700,000 pounds were gone!

33 *The Fall of a Leader*

Each of the six men was as though he had been struck. But with Silver the blow passed almost instantly. Every thought of his soul had been set on that money. Well, he was stopped short. But he kept his head, found his temper, and changed his plan before the others had time to think.

"Jim," he whispered, "take that, and stand by for trouble."

And he passed me a double-barreled pistol.

At the same time he began quietly moving northward, and in a few steps had put the hole between us two and the other five. Then he looked at me and nodded as much as to say, "Here is a tight spot," as, indeed, I thought it was. His looks were now quite friendly. I was so disgusted at these quick changes that I whispered, "So you've changed sides again."

There was no time left for him to answer. The pirates, with oaths and cries, began to leap, one after another, into the pit, and to dig with their fingers, throwing the boards aside as they did so. Morgan found a piece of gold. He held it up with a perfect stream of oaths. It was a two-guinea* piece, and it went from hand to hand among them for a quarter of a minute.

"Two guineas!" roared Merry, shaking it at Silver. "That's your 700,000 pounds, is it? You're the man for bargains, ain't you? You're him that never made mistakes, you wooden-headed fool!"

---

*Guinea: a British unit of money equal to about 5.00 U.S. dollars when this story was written.

"Dig away, boys," said Silver. "You'll find some nuts, I imagine."

"Mates, do you hear that?" screamed Merry. "I tell you now, that man there knew it all along. Look in the face of him, and you'll see it wrote there."

"Ah, Merry," said Silver, "trying to be captain again?"

But this time everyone was entirely on Merry's side. They began to scramble out of the hole, throwing angry glances behind them. One thing I saw, which looked well for us—they all got out upon the far side from Silver.

Well, there we stood, two on one side, five on the other, the pit between us, and nobody with courage enough to strike the first blow. Silver never moved. He watched them, very straight on his crutch, and looked as cool as ever I saw him. He was brave, and no mistake.

At last, Merry seemed to think a speech might help matters.

"Mates," says he, "there's two of them alone there. One's the old one-legged man that brought us all down to this; the other's that cub that I mean to have the heart of. Now, mates—"

He was raising his arm and his voice, and plainly meant to lead a charge. But just then—crack! crack! crack!—three gunshots flashed out of the woods. Merry tumbled head first into the hole. The man with the wounded head spun round like a top and fell all his length upon his side, where he lay dead. The other three turned and ran for it with all their might.

Before you could wink, Long John had fired two barrels of a pistol into the struggling Merry. And as the man rolled up his eyes at him, "George," said he, "I guess I settled you."

At the same moment the doctor, Gray, and Ben Gunn joined us with smoking guns, from among the trees.

"Forward!" cried the doctor. "Double quick, my lads. We must head them off the boats."

And we set off at a great pace, sometimes plunging through the bushes to the chest.

I tell you, Silver was anxious to keep up with us. The work that man did, leaping on his crutch till the muscles of his chest were fit to burst! As it was, he was already 30 yards behind us and just about choking, when we reached the edge of the slope.

"Doctor," he called, "See there! No hurry!"

Sure enough there was no hurry. In a more open part of the woods, we could see the three pirates still running in the same direction as they had started, right for Mizzenmast Hill. We were already between them and the boats. So we four sat down to breathe, while Long John, wiping his face, came slowly up with us.

"Thank ye kindly, doctor," says he. "You came just in time, I guess, for me and Hawkins. And so it's you, Ben Gunn!" he added. "Well, you're a nice one, to be sure."

"I'm Ben Gunn, I am," replied the man of the island, immensely pleased with himself. "And," he added after a long pause, "how do, Mr. Silver? Pretty well, I thank ye, says you."

"Ben, Ben," murmured Silver, "to think as you've beat me!"

The doctor sent Gray back for one of the picks, left behind by the mutineers. Then as we walked easily down hill to where the boats were lying, he told us what had taken place. It was a story that greatly interested Silver; and Ben Gunn was the hero from beginning to end.

Ben, in his long lonely wanderings about the island, had found the skeleton—it was he that had robbed it. He had found the treasure and had dug it up (it was the handle of his pick that lay broken in the hole). He had carried it on his back on many weary trips, from the foot of the tall pine to a cave he had on the hill. There it had lain stored in safety since two months before the arrival of the *Hispaniola*.

The doctor had learned this secret from Ben on the afternoon of the attack. When, next morning, he saw that the *Hispaniola* was gone, he had gone to Silver, given him the chart, which was now useless—given him the stores, for Ben Gunn's cave was well stocked with goats' meat salted by himself—given anything and everything to get a chance of moving in safety from the fort to the hill.

"As for you, Jim," he said, "it went against my heart, but I did what I thought best for those who had stood by their duty. If you were not one of these, whose fault was it?"

That morning, finding that I was to be with the pirates on the treasure hunt, he had run all the way to the cave. Leaving the squire to guard the captain, he had taken Gray and Ben, and started across the island, to be at hand beside the pine. Soon, however, he saw that our party was ahead of him. Ben Gunn, being fleet of foot, had been sent ahead to do his best alone. Then the idea had come to Ben to scare his former shipmates. He was so successful that Gray and the doctor had come up and were already hiding in the woods before the treasure hunters got there.

"Ah," said Silver, "it were lucky for me that I had Hawkins here. You would have let old John be cut to bits, and never given it a thought, Doctor."

"Not a thought," replied Dr. Livesey, cheerfully.

And by this time we had reached the gigs. The doctor, with the pick, broke up one of them, and then we all got aboard the other and set out to go round by sea for North Inlet.

This was a run of eight or nine miles. Silver, though he was already very tired, was set to an oar, like the rest of us, and we were soon gliding swiftly over a smooth sea. Soon we passed out of the straits and doubled the southeast corner of the island, round which, four days ago, we had towed the *Hispaniola*.

As we passed the two-pointed hill, we could see the black mouth of Ben Gunn's cave and a figure standing by it, leaning on a gun. It was the squire. We waved a handkerchief and gave him three cheers, in which the voice of Silver joined as heartily as any.

Three miles farther, just inside the mouth of North Inlet, what should we meet but the *Hispaniola,* sailing by herself! The last tide had lifted her. If there had been much wind or a strong tide current, we should never have found her again. As it was, all was well, except the wreck of the mainsail. We got another anchor ready, and dropped it into the water. We all pulled round again to the nearest point for Ben Gunn's cave. Then Gray, single-handed, returned with the gig to the *Hispaniola,* where he was to pass the night on guard.

A gentle slope ran up from the beach to the mouth of the cave. At the top, the squire met us. He was kind to me, saying nothing of my adventure either in the way of blame or praise.

"John Silver," he said, "you're a rascal and a liar—a liar, sir. I am told I am not to punish you. Well, then, I will not. But the dead men, sir, are a load on your conscience."

"Thank you kindly, sir," replied Long John, again saluting.

"How dare you thank me!" cried the squire. "I should most certainly punish you, if I were not bound by Doctor Livesey's promise. Stand back!"

And then we all went into the cave. It was a large, airy place, with a little spring and a pool of clear water.

The floor was sand. Before a big fire lay Captain Smollett. In a far corner, by the light of the fire, I saw great heaps of coins and bars of gold. That was Flint's treasure that we had come so far to seek, and that had cost already the lives of 17 men from the *Hispaniola*. How many it had cost in gathering it, what blood and sorrow, what good ships sunk on the sea, what brave men murdered, what shot of cannon, what shame and lies and cruelty, perhaps no man alive could tell. Yet there were still three upon that island — Silver, and old Morgan, and Ben Gunn — who had each taken his share in these crimes, as each had hoped in vain to share in the money.

"Come in, Jim," said the captain. "You're a good boy in your line, Jim, but I don't think you and me will go to sea again. You're too much of the born favorite for me. Is that you, John Silver? What brings you here, man?"

"Come back to my duty, sir," returned Silver.

"Ah!" said the captain; and that was all he said.

What a supper I had of it that night, with all my friends around me. What a meal it was, with Ben Gunn's salted goat and a bottle of old wine from the *Hispaniola*. Never, I am sure, were people so gay or so happy. And there was Silver, sitting back almost out of the firelight, but eating heartily, quick to spring forward when anything was wanted, even joining quietly in our laughter — the same mild, polite, humble seaman that he had been on the voyage out.

34 *And Last*

The next morning, we began to work early, for it was a great task to carry all this gold nearly a mile to the beach, and then row it three miles to the *Hispaniola*. The three mutineers still on the island did not greatly trouble us. A single guard on the shoulder of the hill was enough to protect us and we thought, besides, they had had more than enough of fighting.

Therefore, the work was pushed on rapidly. Gray and Ben Gunn came and went with the boat, and the rest, while they were gone, piled treasure on the beach. Two of the bars of gold made a good load for a grown man—one that he was glad to walk slowly with. For my part, as I was not much use at carrying, I was kept busy all day in the cave, packing the money into bread bags.

It was a strange collection, like that in Billy Bones's sea chest, but so much larger and with so many more different kinds of coins. There were English, French, Spanish, and Portuguese coins. There were strange pieces from the East, covered with queer marks, round pieces and square pieces, and pieces with a hole through the middle, as if to wear them round your neck. Nearly every kind of money in the world was in that collection, and so many pieces that my back ached with stooping and my fingers with sorting them out.

Day after day this work went on. By every evening a fortune had been carried aboard, but there was another fortune waiting for the next day. All this time we heard nothing of the three mutineers.

At last—I think it was on the third night—the doctor and I were walking on the shoulder of the hill, when, from out the thick darkness below, the wind brought us a noise between shrieking and singing. It was only a bit that reached our ears, followed by silence.

"Heaven forgive them," said the doctor. "It is the mutineers!"

"All drunk, sir," struck in the voice of Silver from behind us.

Silver, I should say, was given his freedom to move about, and, though everyone was cool to him, he seemed to think himself once more one of us. Indeed, it was surprising how well he bore these slights, and with what politeness he kept on trying to please everyone. Yet, none treated him better than a dog; unless it was Ben Gunn, who was still terribly afraid of him, or myself who really had something to thank him for. Yet, I suppose I had reason to think even worse of him than anybody else. After all I had seen him planning a fresh wickedness upon the hill, when he thought he was going to find the treasure. The doctor answered him shortly.

"Drunk or out of their heads with fever," said he.

"Right you were, sir," replied Silver, "and it makes very little difference to you and me."

"I suppose you would hardly ask me to call you a kind man," returned the doctor, "and so my feelings may surprise you, Master Silver. But if I were sure they were ill—and I am certain one of them is down with fever—I should leave this camp and, at any risk to my own neck, give them all the help I could."

"Ask your pardon, sir, you would be very wrong," said Silver. "You would lose your life, and you may lay to that. I'm on your side now, and I shouldn't wish for our side to lose a man, especially yourself, seeing that I know what I owes you. But these men down there, they couldn't keep their word—no, not even if they wished to. What's more, they couldn't believe that you could."

"No," said the doctor. "You're the man to keep your word, we know that."

Well, that was about the last news we had of the three pirates. Only once we heard a shot a great way off, and thought them to be hunting. We talked it over, and decided that we must desert them on the island—to the huge delight, I must say, of Ben Gunn, and to the satisfaction of Gray. We left a good stock of powder and shot, the most of the salt goat, a few medicines, and some tools, clothing, a spare sail, a length or two of rope, and by the doctor's wishes, a handsome present of tobacco.

That was about the last thing we did on the island. Before that, we had got the treasure loaded, and had stored enough water and the remainder of the goat meat, in case of any trouble at sea. At last, one fine morning, we lifted anchor, which was about all that we could manage, and sailed out of North Inlet. The same colors were flying that the captain had flown and fought under at the fort.

The three fellows must have been watching us closer than we thought, as we soon learned. For, coming through the straits, we had to sail very near the southern point, and there we saw all three of them kneeling together on the point of sand, with their arms raised toward us. It went to all our hearts, I think, to leave them in that wretched state. But we could not risk another mutiny; and to take them home to be hanged would have been a cruel sort of kindness. The doctor called to them and told them of the stores we had left, and where they were to find them. But they went on calling us by name, and begging us to have mercy, and not leave them to die in such a place.

At last, seeing the ship still went on her course and was now swiftly drawing out of hearing, one of them—I know not which it was—jumped to his feet. With a loud cry, he whipped his gun to his shoulder, and sent a shot whistling over Silver's head and through the mainsail.

After that, we kept out of their sight, and when next I looked out they had left the point, and the point itself had almost melted out of sight in the distance. That was the end of that. Before noon, to my great joy, the highest rock of Treasure Island had sunk into the blue round of sea.

We were so short of men that everyone on board had to lend a hand—only the captain lying on a cot on deck and giving his orders. For, though almost well, he must still be quiet. We sailed for the nearest port in Spanish America, for we could not risk the voyage home without fresh hands. As it was, what with strong winds and a couple of fresh storms, we were all worn out before we reached it.

It was just sundown when we cast anchor in a beautiful gulf. At once we were surrounded by shore boats full of blacks and Mexican Indians selling fruits and vegetables, and offering to dive for bits of money. The sight of so many good-humored faces, the taste of the fruits, and above all, the lights that began to shine in the town, were pleasantly different from our dark and bloody stay on the island. The doctor and the squire, taking me along with them, went ashore to pass the early part of the night. Here they met the captain of an English vessel, went on board his ship, and had so pleasant a time that day was breaking when we came alongside the *Hispaniola*.

Ben Gunn was on deck alone, and, as soon as we came on board, he began to tell us the news. Silver was gone. Ben Gunn, himself, had helped him to escape in a shore boat some hours ago. He now told us he had only done so to save our lives, which would certainly have been lost if "that man with the one leg had stayed aboard." But this was not all. Old John Silver had not gone empty-handed. He had cut through a wall and had taken one of the sacks of coin, worth perhaps 300 or 400 guineas, to help him on his wanderings.

I think we were all pleased to be rid of him so easily.

Well, to make a long story short, we got a few hands on board, made a good cruise home, and the *Hispaniola* reached Bristol just as Mr. Blandly was beginning to think of fitting out a ship to look for us. Five men only of those who had sailed returned with her. "Drink and the devil had done for the rest," although, to be sure, we were not quite in so bad a case as that other ship they sang about:

> "With one man of her crew alive,
> What put to sea with seventy-five."

All of us had a generous share of the treasure, and used it wisely or foolishly, as we chose. Captain Smollett is now retired from the sea. Gray not only saved his money, but studied his work. He is now mate and part owner of a fine ship; married besides, and the father of a family. As for Ben Gunn, he got 1,000 pounds, which he spent or lost in three weeks, or, to be more exact, in 19 days, for he was back begging on the twentieth. Then he was given a place as a gatekeeper, exactly as he had feared upon the island. He still lives, a great favorite, though something of a joke among the country boys, and a fine singer in church on Sundays and saints' days.

Of Silver we have heard no more. That fearful seaman with one leg has at last gone clean out of my life. But I suppose he met his old wife, and perhaps still lives in comfort with her and his parrot, Captain Flint. It is to be hoped so, I suppose, for his chances of comfort in another world are very small.

The bar silver and the arms still lie, for all that I know, where Flint buried them. Certainly they shall lie there for all of me. Nothing would ever bring me back again to that terrible island. The worst dreams that ever I have are when I hear the waves roaring about its coasts, or start upright in bed, with the sharp voice of Captain Flint still ringing in my ears, "Pieces of eight! Pieces of eight!"

The End

REVIEWING YOUR READING

CHAPTER 1

FINDING THE IMPORTANT IDEA

1. This chapter is mostly about how
(A) the narrator's father becomes deathly ill (B) the
captain spends his time at the inn (C) Dr. Livesey
threatens to have the captain arrested (D) the captain
doesn't pay the money he owes

REMEMBERING DETAIL

2. The captain tells the narrator to
(A) carry his sea chest to his room (B) heat his rum in
a silver cup (C) give a secret message to Dr. Livesey
(D) watch out for a one-legged seaman

DRAWING CONCLUSIONS

3. You can tell from the chapter that the captain
(A) is an old friend of Dr. Livesey's (B) is really a
soldier in disguise (C) believes someone is looking for
him (D) believes the inn is haunted

USING YOUR REASON

4. The captain was a "real old salt." This means he
(A) was a true seagoing man (B) used to be a cook
(C) never set foot on a ship in his life (D) was not a
drinking man

IDENTIFYING THE MOOD

5. After Dr. Livesey warns the captain to behave himself,
the captain probably feels
(A) timid (B) angry (C) happy (D) brave

6. How did the other visitors to the inn feel about the
captain?
(A) They ignored him. (B) They loved him like a
father. (C) They were frightened of him. (D) They
thought he was funny and harmless.

THINKING IT OVER

1. Try to describe the narrator. How old was he when the story took place? What kind of person does he seem to be? What makes you think so?

2. What do you learn about the captain's past? Why do you think he wishes to avoid other seamen? What secrets do you think he may have?

CHAPTER 2

FINDING THE BEST TITLE

1. Which title tells most about the chapter?
(A) Black Dog's Rum (B) A Bitter Cold Winter
(C) Dr. Livesey Comes Just in Time (D) The Captain Fights and Falls

REMEMBERING DETAIL

2. All of the following are true about Black Dog EXCEPT
(A) he wears a cutlass (B) he has been to sea (C) one of his legs is missing (D) two of his fingers are missing

3. The captain and Black Dog
(A) don't know each other (B) have an argument and a fight (C) are happy to see each other (D) promise to see each other again soon

4. What happens to the captain?
(A) He has a stroke. (B) He is killed. (C) He is wounded. (D) He goes insane.

DRAWING CONCLUSIONS

5. You can determine that the narrator's name is
(A) Billy Bones (B) Jim Hawkins (C) Dr. Livesey
(D) Admiral Benbow

USING YOUR REASON

6. By saying that Black Dog "showed his heels," the author means that Black Dog
(A) ran away (B) kicked the captain (C) needed his boots repaired (D) was low-down and mean

IDENTIFYING THE MOOD

7. How does Dr. Livesey feel about the captain at the end of the chapter?
(A) He feels sorry for him. (B) He is annoyed at him.
(C) He would like to be the captain's friend. (D) He is happy he saved the captain's life.

READING FOR DEEPER MEANING

8. Which of the following best describes Black Dog's relationship with the captain?
   (A) Envy (B) Fondness (C) Trust (D) Fear

THINKING IT OVER

1. Describe the look on the captain's face when he first sees Black Dog. What do you suppose he is thinking?
2. What do you think Black Dog and the captain talk about? Why would it lead to a fight? Try to think of some good ideas as to what their talk might be about.

CHAPTER 3

FINDING THE BEST TITLE

1. Which title tells most about the chapter?
   (A) Death Strikes Twice (B) One Glass of Rum
   (C) Black Dog Returns (D) The Blind Man's Laughter

REMEMBERING DETAIL

2. In this chapter, Jim Hawkins's father
   (A) runs away (B) goes blind (C) kills the captain
   (D) dies

DRAWING CONCLUSIONS

3. You can conclude that the blind man and his friends want to
   (A) get the captain's money (B) take the captain to sea (C) hang the captain (D) leave the captain alone

USING YOUR REASON

4. The blind man's purpose in coming to the inn is to
   (A) look for Black Dog (B) ask the captain to join his crew (C) find out who Jim Hawkins is (D) give the captain a warning
5. Which of the following best describes the character of the blind man?
   (A) Timid (B) Evil (C) Courteous (D) Unfriendly

THINKING IT OVER

1. Jim says he never liked the captain. But why do you think Jim starts to cry at the captain's death?
2. Reread what Jim says about the blind man. What is so horrible about him? How does the captain react when he sees the blind man?
3. What is terror? Why does the blind man seem so much more terrible than Black Dog?

CHAPTER 4

FINDING THE IMPORTANT IDEA

1. The author is mostly interested in telling how
   (A) the fog creeps in over the harbor (B) Jim and his mother leave the inn, return, and leave again (C) Jim and his mother hide under a bridge (D) the people of the village help Jim and his mother

REMEMBERING DETAIL

2. Who accompanies Jim and his mother back to the inn?
   (A) No one (B) Mrs. Crossley (C) Only one old man
   (D) Four men from the village
3. Who comes to the inn while Jim and his mother are inside?
   (A) Black Dog (B) Dr. Livesey (C) The blind man
   (D) Two men from the village
4. Besides some gold, what does Jim take from the captain's sea chest?
   (A) A piece of silver (B) Two pairs of pistols (C) A pair of compasses (D) An oilskin package
5. The Hawkinses return to the inn in order to
   (A) bury the dead captain properly (B) lock the door to keep strangers out (C) get the money that is owed to them (D) wait for Black Dog

IDENTIFYING THE MOOD

6. What is Jim's feeling when he hears the tapping on the road?
   (A) Joy (B) Fear (C) Sadness (D) Anger

THINKING IT OVER

1. Jim's mother is very honest. How do you know? Do you think she is wise in being so honest considering the circumstances? Why or why not?

CHAPTER 5

FINDING THE IMPORTANT IDEA

1. The important idea of the chapter is that
(A) the blind man cannot trust his friends (B) the inn
is ruined by the pirates (C) the pirates are after
something other than the captain's gold (D) Jim and
his mother are rescued in the nick of time

REMEMBERING DETAILS

2. When they get to the inn, the pirates realize that
(A) the captain is not really dead (B) the officers have
been there before them (C) the captain's sea chest has
already been searched (D) Jim and his mother are
hiding under the bridge

3. Pew, the blind man, dies when
(A) Black Dog stabs him (B) he is shot by an officer
(C) he drowns while swimming after the boat (D) he is
trampled by a horse

DRAWING CONCLUSIONS

4. You can tell that the papers in Jim's pocket are
(A) valuable documents (B) pages from a Spanish
book (C) worthless trash (D) old love letters

USING YOUR REASON

5. Jim's reason for going to Dr. Livesey is to
(A) hide from the pirates (B) give the papers to him
(C) get medical treatment for his mother (D) tell him
that the captain is dead

READING FOR DEEPER MEANING

6. The way the pirates act toward each other suggests that
(A) shipmates are like brothers (B) all men are
basically honest (C) nobody is as bad as he seems
(D) there is no honor among thieves

THINKING IT OVER

1. What do you learn about the papers that Jim has taken
from the captain's chest? What do you think the
papers are?

CHAPTER 6

FINDING THE IMPORTANT IDEA

1. The author is mostly interested in telling how
(A) Jim eats a hearty supper (B) the treasure map is
discovered (C) Jim and Mr. Dance ride to the squire's
house (D) Mr. Dance tells the story of the evening's
events

REMEMBERING DETAIL

2. Who was Captain Flint?
(A) The squire's cousin (B) A wealthy landowner
(C) A soldier (D) A pirate
3. The squire and Dr. Livesey decide to
(A) send Jim back to his mother (B) outfit a ship to
find the treasure (C) tell Mr. Dance all their plans
(D) join up with the pirates and go to sea

DRAWING CONCLUSIONS

4. You can tell that Dr. Livesey thinks
(A) the pirates will try to follow them (B) the treasure
map is a fake (C) the squire is a foolish man (D) Jim
would be useless on a sea voyage

USING YOUR REASON

5. When the doctor tells the squire to "hold his tongue," he
means that the squire must
(A) keep his pistol ready (B) stop drinking (C) keep
silent (D) go on a diet
6. Which of the following best describes the character of
the squire?
(A) Quiet (B) Unfriendly (C) High-spirited
(D) Deceitful

THINKING IT OVER

1. What does the captain's book tell you about the kind of
life he had led?
2. Why is it so important that everything be done in secret?
Do you think Jim, Dr. Livesey, and Squire Trelawney will
be able to keep their plans secret? Why or why not?

3. Compare the personalities of Dr. Livesey and Squire Trelawney. Who is the more level-headed? Who is the more outgoing? Which type of personality do you prefer? Why?

CHAPTER 7

FINDING THE BEST TITLE
1. Which tells most about the chapter?
(A) The Ship Is Ready (B) A Good Cook (C) Jim's Wonderful Dreams (D) Tom Redruth's Complaint

REMEMBERING DETAIL
2. The name of the ship is the
(A) *Blandly* (B) *Spyglass* (C) *Bristol* (D) *Hispaniola*
3. All of the following are true about Long John Silver EXCEPT
(A) he has only one leg (B) he will be the ship's cook
(C) he has no money (D) he helped Squire Trelawney gather the crew

DRAWING CONCLUSIONS
4. You can conclude from the chapter that Squire Trelawney has probably
(A) talked too much (B) bought a bad ship (C) stolen some money (D) argued with Dr. Livesey

USING YOUR REASON
5. When Jim says he "slept like a log," he means he
(A) didn't sleep well (B) slept soundly (C) had bad dreams (D) fell asleep beside a tree

IDENTIFYING THE MOOD
6. Squire Trelawney's letter shows that he feels
(A) tired (B) excited (C) worried (D) lonesome

THINKING IT OVER
1. Very often you can learn more from what is not said than from what is said. Notice that Squire Trelawney's letter says a lot about Silver, the ship's cook, but very little about the man who will be captain of the ship. What do

you learn about Silver? What do you learn about the captain?

2. Explain the importance of the crew on such a voyage. What do you know about the crew that has been hired?

CHAPTER 8

FINDING THE BEST TITLE

1. Which title tells most about the chapter?
(A) Jim Meets Long John Silver (B) Black Dog Returns (C) Jim Walks the Docks (D) John Silver Laughs

REMEMBERING DETAIL

2. Who does Jim see in John Silver's inn?
(A) Pew, the blind man (B) Bill Bones (C) Black Dog
(D) Dr. Livesey

DRAWING CONCLUSIONS

3. You can conclude from the chapter that Long John Silver
(A) is afraid of Black Dog (B) has been an admiral in the navy (C) is a relative of Dr. Livesey's (D) is not as honest as he seems to be

USING YOUR REASON

4. John Silver's reason for going to Squire Trelawney is to
(A) bring him a pint of rum (B) make sure that Jim gets back safely (C) explain why Black Dog was able to escape (D) tell him what supplies he'll need on the ship

IDENTIFYING THE MOOD

5. At the end of the chapter, Dr. Livesey
(A) likes John Silver (B) distrusts John Silver
(C) hates John Silver (D) distrusts Jim Hawkins

THINKING IT OVER

1. What do you learn about the character of Long John Silver? Would you trust him? Why or why not?

2. How does the incident of Black Dog's escape raise suspicions about John Silver? Does anything else raise suspicions about him?

CHAPTER 9

FINDING THE IMPORTANT IDEA

1. This chapter is mostly about
   (A) Squire Trelawney's anger with Captain Smollett
   (B) Captain Smollett's feelings about the trip
   (C) Mr. Arrow's drinking with the crew   (D) John
   Silver's preparations for dinner

REMEMBERING DETAIL

2. Captain Smollett is worried for all these reasons EXCEPT
   (A) all the crew knows more than he does   (B) the
   Hispaniola seems to be an unsafe ship   (C) voyages for
   treasure are dangerous   (D) the powder and arms are
   stored near the crew

DRAWING CONCLUSIONS

3. You can tell that the one person who is happy with
   Captain Smollett is
   (A) Dr. Livesey   (B) Jim   (C) Squire Trelawney
   (D) John Silver

USING YOUR REASON

4. When Captain Smollett says, "The secret has been told
   to the parrot," he means
   (A) the secret is safe   (B) he wants no parrots on board
   his ship   (C) the crew is an excellent group of men
   (D) the secret is no longer secret

5. Which of the following best describes the character of
   Captain Smollett?
   (A) Happy and carefree   (B) Quiet and gentle
   (C) Honest and blunt   (D) Deceitful and shifty

THINKING IT OVER

1. Why do you suppose Captain Smollett doesn't trust the
   crew? Why do you think he insists on changing the
   location of the powder and the arms?

2. If Squire Trelawney hasn't "blabbed" about the treasure
   map, how do you suppose the story of the map has
   gotten around to so many people?

CHAPTER 10

FINDING THE BEST TITLE

1. Which title tells most about the chapter?
   (A) Long John's Songs (B) The Disappearance of
   Mr. Arrow (C) The Handsome Parrot (D) Dangerous
   Words Overheard

REMEMBERING DETAIL

2. What was the problem with the first mate, Mr. Arrow?
   (A) He drank too much. (B) He had a bad leg. (C) He
   overworked the men. (D) He threatened the men with
   his sword.

3. At the end of the chapter, Jim is hiding
   (A) behind the parrot's cage (B) in the captain's
   quarters (C) among the guns and powder (D) in the
   apple barrel

DRAWING CONCLUSIONS

4. You can conclude that what Jim overhears
   (A) is none of his business (B) shows that John Silver
   is an honest man (C) reveals John Silver to be evil
   (D) is the parrot's voice and nothing more

USING YOUR REASON

5. When the captain says, "Spoil the ship's hands, make
   devils," he means
   (A) the "hands" of a ship are really its sails (B) if you
   treat the crew too well, they will take advantage of you
   (C) the devil can always find a way to get on board a
   ship (D) the men will work harder if they get double
   portions of rum

IDENTIFYING THE MOOD

6. How do the men feel as the ship nears Treasure Island?
   (A) Sad (B) Happy (C) Secretive (D) Greedy

READING FOR DEEPER MEANING

7. Which of the following best describes the relationship
   between Captain Smollett and Squire Trelawney?
   (A) Admiration (B) Trust (C) Dislike
   (D) Brotherliness

242

THINKING IT OVER

1. What do you suppose happened to Mr. Arrow? Why didn't anyone care?
2. At the end of the chapter, Jim says, "For from these dozen words, I understood that the lives of all the honest men aboard depended upon me alone." What do you think Jim has heard?

CHAPTER 11

FINDING THE BEST TITLE

1. Which title tells most about the chapter?
   (A) A Drink of Rum (B) John Silver's Plans (C) The Story of Israel Hands (D) Young Dick Becomes a Pirate

REMEMBERING DETAIL

2. According to John Silver, where are most of Captain Flint's men?
   (A) Dead and buried (B) In Bristol's jails (C) At Treasure Island (D) On board the *Hispaniola*
3. What does Silver want to do with the "honest men" on the *Hispaniola*?
   (A) Kill them (B) Sell them as slaves (C) Return them to Bristol (D) Leave them on an island
4. John Silver's main reason for not taking over the ship right away is that he
   (A) likes Squire Trelawney (B) knows Jim is overhearing him (C) needs Captain Smollett to steer the ship (D) is afraid of Israel Hands

DRAWING CONCLUSIONS

5. John Silver won't return to Bristol after this cruise because he knows
   (A) he'll be dead (B) his wife will try to kill him
   (C) Captain Flint will be there (D) the law will be after him

IDENTIFYING THE MOOD

6. Which of the following best describes the character of Israel Hands?
   (A) Sober (B) Strict (C) Impatient (D) Religious

READING FOR DEEPER MEANING

7. John Silver would most agree with which of the following?

(A) Live for today. (B) Haste makes waste. (C) Love your enemy. (D) One pirate can always trust another.

THINKING IT OVER

1. Explain in detail John Silver's reasons for not taking over the ship right away. Imagine you are a pirate. Are Silver's reasons good? Why or why not?

2. You now know the truth about John Silver. How do you think Silver has been able to hide his true nature from Jim, Dr. Livesey, and Squire Trelawney?

CHAPTER 12

FINDING THE IMPORTANT IDEA

1. The author is mostly interested in telling how
   (A) John Silver tries to win Jim's trust again (B) all the sailors receive a serving of rum (C) the ship comes near to Treasure Island (D) Jim reveals Silver's plans to Captain Smollett, Dr. Livesey, and Squire Trelawney

REMEMBERING DETAIL

2. The main hill on Treasure Island is named
   (A) Foremast Hill (B) Skeleton Hill (C) Captain Kidd's Hill (D) Spyglass Hill

DRAWING CONCLUSIONS

3. Silver is disappointed when he looks at Captain Smollett's map because
   (A) it is not the treasure map (B) it shows a harbor on the south of Treasure Island (C) he realizes that they have come to the wrong island (D) it does not show the current that runs up the island's west coast

USING YOUR REASON

4. The captain orders that the sailors receive a serving of rum. He does this in order to
   (A) reward them (B) distract them (C) show the men how generous he is (D) get rid of the rum before going on the island

IDENTIFYING THE MOOD

5. After Squire Trelawney finds out about Silver's plans, how does he act toward Captain Smollett?
   (A) Angry (B) Apologetic (C) Distrustful (D) Fearful

THINKING IT OVER

1. The captain says that this is the first time he's ever seen a crew which had mutiny in mind but which had given no signs of it. Dr. Livesey answers "That's Silver. A very remarkable man." Explain the doctor's answer.
2. What plans do Captain Smollett, Dr. Livesey, and Squire Trelawney make to deal with the mutineers? Why are they counting on Jim so much?

CHAPTER 13

FINDING THE IMPORTANT IDEA

1. The chapter is mostly about how
(A) the men are allowed to go ashore and Jim goes with them (B) Dr. Livesey decides that there is sickness on Treasure Island (C) the men decide to mutiny in spite of John Silver (D) the *Hispaniola* is anchored near Skeleton Island

REMEMBERING DETAIL

2. The air around the harbor smells of
(A) rotting plant life (B) fresh flowers (C) oil and gasoline (D) burning wood
3. The captain gives a loaded pistol to
(A) John Silver (B) each of the trustworthy seamen
(C) everyone except Hunter, Joyce, and Redruth
(D) Jim Hawkins only

DRAWING CONCLUSIONS

4. You can tell that Jim's going ashore will
(A) result in his death (B) turn out to be a good idea
(C) turn out to be a foolish idea (D) result in the death of Squire Trelawney

USING YOUR REASON

5. Captain Smollet sends the men ashore because he knows that
(A) they will not return (B) they will get sick in the swamps (C) John Silver will try to calm them down
(D) they will find the treasure

IDENTIFYING THE MOOD

6. How does Jim feel as he first looks upon Treasure Island from the ship?
   (A) Glad (B) Anxious (C) Proud (D) Unhappy

THINKING IT OVER

1. As Jim races into the bushes, he hears John Silver calling him. Why do you think Jim doesn't answer? What do you think Silver wants?

CHAPTER 14

FINDING THE IMPORTANT IDEA

1. The author is mostly interested in telling how
   (A) Jim explores the island (B) Alan dies (C) Jim realizes his life is in danger (D) Tom decides to join up with Silver

REMEMBERING DETAIL

2. At the end of the chapter, Tom is
   (A) killed by Silver (B) hiding with Jim (C) swimming toward the *Hispaniola* (D) searching for the treasure

DRAWING CONCLUSIONS

3. You can conclude that Alan was killed because he
   (A) planned to sink the *Hispaniola* (B) wanted to join the pirates (C) knew where the treasure was
   (D) refused to join the pirates

USING YOUR REASON

4. When Jim hears the pirates shouting, he says, "This sound of danger lent me wings." By this Jim means
   (A) his fear made him run away fast (B) birds warned him that he was in danger (C) he was so happy he felt he could fly (D) he was not afraid of them

IDENTIFYING THE MOOD

5. As Jim runs, he feels
   (A) happy (B) hopeless (C) angry (D) confident

THINKING IT OVER

1. Jim witnesses a murder. How does he react? What are his thoughts as he watches the murderer, Silver, clean his knife?
2. Explain the dilemma that Jim is in at the end of the chapter. Why does he believe that he can't return to the boats? Yet what would it mean if he didn't return?

CHAPTER 15

FINDING THE IMPORTANT IDEA

1. The chapter is mostly about
   (A) the fight between the "good men" and the pirates
   (B) the gun Jim has in his pocket   (C) Jim's meeting Ben Gunn   (D) Jim's exploring the island

REMEMBERING DETAIL

2. How long has Ben Gunn been on the island?
   (A) Six months   (B) Three years   (C) Ten years
   (D) He doesn't say
3. What food has Ben Gunn missed most?
   (A) Cheese   (B) Berries   (C) Goat meat   (D) Fish

DRAWING CONCLUSIONS

4. You can tell from the chapter that Ben Gunn
   (A) was never a pirate   (B) wants to stay on the island
   (C) is a friend of Long John Silver's   (D) has found the treasure

USING YOUR REASON

5. Which of the following best describes the character of Ben Gunn?
   (A) Cunning but friendly   (B) Greedy and murderous
   (C) Hateful but religious   (D) Foolish and evil

THINKING IT OVER

1. Why do you think Jim decides to trust Ben Gunn? Do you think Ben is trustworthy? Why or why not?
2. Explain the deal that Ben Gunn wishes to make with Squire Trelawney.

CHAPTER 16

FINDING THE IMPORTANT IDEA

1. This chapter is mostly about how
(A) the "good men" leave the *Hispaniola* (B) Abraham Gray joins the "good men" (C) Silver's men try to kill Dr. Livesey (D) the pirates on board try to take over the ship

REMEMBERING DETAIL

2. The first time Dr. Livesey goes ashore, he
(A) can't find the fort (B) whistles "Lillibullero" as a signal (C) sees John Silver hiding in the woods (D) hears a man's death cry
3. Who guards the gallery on the ship?
(A) Abraham Gray (B) Israel Hands (C) Hunter (D) Redruth

DRAWING CONCLUSIONS

4. You can tell that Abraham Gray is a good man because he
(A) tries to kill John Silver (B) is upset when he hears the death cry (C) follows Israel Hands (D) stays on board the ship

USING YOUR REASON

5. Dr. Livesey says that while rowing, he and Hunter "Made the water fly." By this he means
(A) their boat sank (B) their oars broke and they rowed with their hands (C) they rowed fast (D) they caught a water fly

READING FOR DEEPER MEANING

6. Which of the following best describes Abraham Gray's relationship to Captain Smollett?
(A) Fear (B) Hatred (C) Loyalty (D) Love

THINKING IT OVER

1. When Dr. Livesey hears the death cry, he thinks it is Jim Hawkins. How do you know it isn't Jim?
2. Why does Captain Smollett challenge the pirates who stay on the ship? Does his challenge work?

CHAPTER 17

FINDING THE BEST TITLE

1. Which title tells most about the chapter?
   (A) Man Overboard (B) The Ship's Gun Roars (C) A
   Short but Dangerous Journey (D) "Keep Your
   Powder Dry!"

REMEMBERING DETAIL

2. All of these are true about the jolly-boat EXCEPT
   (A) it flies the pirate flag (B) it has trouble fighting the
   current (C) it is overloaded (D) it finally sinks
3. Squire Trelawney shoots his gun and hits
   (A) nothing (B) Israel Hands (C) Abraham Gray
   (D) one of the pirates on the *Hispaniola*
4. Captain Smollett will not row any harder because
   (A) he is too tired (B) he is angry about having to row
   (C) strong rowing might sink the jolly-boat (D) the
   current keeps the boat going east

USING YOUR REASON

5. Dr. Livesey seems to feel that Abraham Gray is
   (A) wise beyond measure (B) impolite (C) sinister
   (D) trustworthy

THINKING IT OVER

1. Do you think it was wise to have left the *Hispaniola* in
   the hands of the pirates? Why or why not?
2. Where is Jim Hawkins and what is he doing while all
   this is happening? How do you know?

CHAPTER 18

FINDING THE IMPORTANT IDEA

1. This chapter is mostly about
   (A) Tom Redruth's death (B) Jim Hawkins's return
   (C) what takes place on the *Hispaniola* (D) what takes
   place at the fort

REMEMBERING DETAIL

2. How many of the pirates die in this chapter?
   (A) None (B) One (C) Two (D) Three

DRAWING CONCLUSIONS

3. Until Jim returns, you can conclude that Dr. Livesey thinks Jim has

(A) drowned (B) met Ben Gunn (C) been killed by the pirates (D) joined the pirates

USING YOUR REASON

4. When the author says the captain had "run up the colors," he means the captain had

(A) raised the British flag (B) run away from the fort (C) gotten sick at the sight of blood (D) washed his clothes

IDENTIFYING THE MOOD

5. How does Dr. Livesey feel when he sees Abraham Gray take up his cutlass?

(A) Encouraged (B) Frightened (C) Worried (D) Angry

READING FOR DEEPER MEANING

6. According to Captain Smollett, Tom Redruth's death shows that

(A) only cowards live to an old age (B) pirates are made, not born (C) it is noble to die in the line of duty (D) death comes when one least expects it

THINKING IT OVER

1. Jim Hawkins narrated the first 15 chapters of the book. Why has there been a different narrator for the last three chapters?

2. How does Squire Trelawney react to Tom Redruth's death? How does Captain Smollett react? Why might they react so differently?

CHAPTER 19

FINDING THE BEST TITLE

1. Which title tells most about the chapter?

(A) Ben Gunn Makes a Bargain (B) Hawkins Returns to the Fort (C) Silver Waves a Flag of Truce (D) The Pirates Capture the Fort

REMEMBERING DETAIL

2. What is the Jolly Roger?
   (A) A song the pirates sing   (B) An inn in Bristol
   (C) The name of the pirates' boat   (D) The pirates' flag
3. Inside the fort, Captain Smollett tries to
   (A) kill Ben Gunn   (B) tie up Abraham Gray   (C) keep
   the men's spirits up   (D) bury the map in a corner

DRAWING CONCLUSIONS

4. You can conclude that during the night Ben Gunn will
   try to
   (A) kill some of the pirates   (B) sink the *Hispaniola*
   (C) get to the fort   (D) find the treasure map

USING YOUR REASON

5. Ben Gunn doesn't go to the fort with Jim because he
   (A) wants to know first if Squire Trelawney will accept
   his bargain   (B) knows that Captain Smollett will kill
   him   (C) thinks that John Silver is inside the fort
   (D) thinks that Jim is a liar

IDENTIFYING THE MOOD

6. Captain Smollett, Squire Trelawney, and Dr. Livesey all
   feel that their chances of surviving
   (A) are excellent   (B) are completely hopeless   (C) are
   bad but not hopeless   (D) depend completely upon
   Ben Gunn

THINKING IT OVER

1. What do the men in the fort have going for them? What
   do the men in the fort have working against them?
2. At the end of the chapter, John Silver approaches with a
   flag of truce. Imagine you are Silver. What reason would
   you have to come with a flag of truce? What would you
   say to the men in the fort?

CHAPTER 20

FINDING THE IMPORTANT IDEA

1. This chapter is mostly about
   (A) Silver's offer and Captain Smollett's reply
   (B) Silver's desire to join up with the good men   (C) the
   man who was killed during the night   (D) the treasure
   and where it is hidden

REMEMBERING DETAIL

2. The morning on the island is
   (A) rainy and foggy (B) warm and clear (C) sunny and dry (D) cold and damp
3. Silver asks Captain Smollett for the treasure map. What does Silver promise in return?
   (A) Food and wine (B) Safety (C) Half the treasure (D) A decent burial

DRAWING CONCLUSIONS

4. You can tell from the chapter that Ben Gunn has
   (A) joined the pirates (B) killed one of the pirates (C) sunk the *Hispaniola* (D) left the island for good

USING YOUR REASON

5. When the author says Silver "was tricked out in his best," he means
   (A) Silver was tricked by the captain (B) Silver's trick worked best (C) Silver was wearing his best clothes (D) Silver was pretending he didn't need his crutch

THINKING IT OVER

1. Why do you think John Silver makes his offer?
2. How does Captain Smollett respond to Silver's offer? What reasons does he give?
3. Why don't the men in the fort kill Silver when they have the chance? How do you think the pirates would act in the same situation? How do you know?

CHAPTER 21

FINDING THE IMPORTANT IDEA

1. The chapter is mostly about
   (A) Ben Gunn's plan (B) the death of Joyce (C) the battle at the fort (D) John Silver's return to his men

REMEMBERING DETAIL

2. During the fight, Jim is cut
   (A) on his cheek (B) near his knee (C) across his fingers (D) on top of his shoulder
3. Who kills Job Anderson?
   (A) Jim (B) Abraham Gray (C) Dr. Livesey (D) Squire Trelawney

4. How many pirates die during the fight?
(A) None (B) One (C) Four (D) Five

USING YOUR REASON
5. When the author says two pirates had "bit the dust," he means they had
(A) surrendered (B) been killed (C) run away
(D) been wounded

IDENTIFYING THE MOOD
6. At the end of the chapter, Captain Smollett feels
(A) hopeful (B) hopeless (C) angry (D) jealous

THINKING IT OVER
1. In what ways does Captain Smollett show his abilities as a leader?
2. What part does Jim play in the battle? Has he been an effective fighter? Explain your answer.
3. At the end of the chapter, what does Captain Smollett think of his men's chances of winning? Do you agree with him? Why or why not?

CHAPTER 22

FINDING THE BEST TITLE
1. Which title tells most about the chapter?
(A) Outside the Fort (B) The Captain's Wounds
(C) Dr. Livesey's Trip (D) The Parrot's Screams

REMEMBERING DETAIL
2. Jim guesses that Dr. Livesey has gone off to
(A) see Ben Gunn (B) get food (C) kill John Silver
(D) sink the *Hispaniola*
3. After finding Ben Gunn's boat, Jim decides to
(A) go back to the fort (B) sleep under the trees
(C) cut the *Hispaniola* loose (D) sink the *Hispaniola*

DRAWING CONCLUSIONS
4. When his friends find out that Jim is gone, you can conclude that they will be
(A) lonely (B) uncaring (C) happy (D) angry

USING YOUR REASON

5. After Dr. Livesey patches Jim's wounds, why does he pull Jim's ears?
(A) To show fondness (B) To punish him (C) To help him hear better (D) To warn him about Ben Gunn

IDENTIFYING THE MOOD

6. Jim's behavior in this chapter shows that he is
(A) headstrong (B) cowardly (C) obedient
(D) carefree

THINKING IT OVER

1. Jim may not have been much help during the battle, but how has he helped his friends in other ways? How does he think he can help them in this chapter?
2. Was it wise of Jim to leave the fort? Why or why not?
3. What do you think Dr. Livesey will discuss with Ben Gunn?

CHAPTER 23

FINDING THE BEST TITLE

1. Which title tells most about the chapter?
(A) A Bottle of Rum (B) The *Hispaniola* Is Loose
(C) The Campfire on Shore (D) Jim Paddles to Safety

REMEMBERING DETAIL

2. Jim says that Ben Gunn's boat is
(A) safe for him (B) too large for him (C) easy to handle (D) sure to sink
3. The two pirates on the *Hispaniola* do all of these things EXCEPT
(A) drink (B) quarrel (C) fight (D) sing

USING YOUR REASON

4. Jim doesn't cut the anchor rope right away because
(A) he's afraid he'll be seen (B) he can't find it (C) it is too tightly stretched (D) it is too thick

READING FOR DEEPER MEANING

5. The story suggests that the pirates' worst enemy is
(A) fire (B) the sea (C) the weather (D) themselves

THINKING IT OVER

1. Discuss the characters of the pirates. What sort of fighters have they been? Why do you think they've done so poorly?
2. What are Jim's feelings as the chapter ends? Do you think he regrets what he has done? Why or why not?

CHAPTER 24

FINDING THE BEST TITLE

1. Which title tells most about the chapter?
   (A) Morning Comes (B) The Cape of the Woods
   (C) Sea Lions Near the Shore (D) Catching the *Hispaniola*

REMEMBERING DETAIL

2. When Jim first wakes up, how far is he from shore?
   (A) Fifty yards (B) A quarter mile (C) Two miles
   (D) Too far to tell
3. Jim finds that his little boat moves safely if he
   (A) stands up in it (B) paddles steadily (C) stays still and low (D) moves from side to side

DRAWING CONCLUSIONS

4. You can figure out that if the wind and the current had come from opposite directions,
   (A) the *Hispaniola* would have sunk (B) the pirates would have seen Jim (C) Jim could have swum to shore (D) Jim would have drowned

USING YOUR REASON

5. Jim's reason for boarding the *Hispaniola* is to
   (A) kill the two men on board (B) return the ship to Captain Smollett (C) avoid the sea lions at the shore (D) keep his little boat from sinking

IDENTIFYING THE MOOD

6. How does Jim feel as the *Hispaniola* comes toward him?
   (A) Frightened (B) Joyful (C) Unhappy (D) Proud

THINKING IT OVER

1. In what ways does Jim show his initiative in this chapter? How does his quick thinking save his life?

CHAPTER 25

FINDING THE IMPORTANT IDEA
1. The author is mostly interested in telling how
   (A) Israel Hands almost dies (B) Jim takes charge of
   the ship (C) Jim searches the ship for the map
   (D) Jim takes down the Jolly Roger

REMEMBERING DETAIL
2. Whom does Jim find on the deck of the *Hispaniola*?
   (A) Israel Hands and the red-capped sailor (B) John
   Silver (C) Ben Gunn (D) Captain Smollett and
   Dr. Livesey
3. Where does Jim intend to take the *Hispaniola*?
   (A) Haulbowline Head (B) Captain Kidd's Harbor
   (C) Skeleton Island (D) The North Inlet

DRAWING CONCLUSIONS
4. You can conclude that the sailor in the red cap has
   (A) died from sickness (B) been killed by an accident
   (C) been killed by Israel Hands (D) been killed by Jim
   Hawkins

USING YOUR REASON
5. When Jim says the sight of Israel Hands "went right to
   my heart," he means
   (A) he felt sorry for Hands (B) he didn't care about
   Hands's suffering (C) Hands tried to shoot him through
   the heart (D) Hands seemed sad and lonely

IDENTIFYING THE MOOD
6. How does Jim feel about Israel Hands watching him?
   (A) Happy (B) Angry (C) Confident (D) Uneasy

THINKING IT OVER
1. What bargain does Israel Hands propose to Jim? Why
   does Jim decide to accept it?
2. Explain Jim's conflicting feelings at the end of the
   chapter.

CHAPTER 26

FINDING THE BEST TITLE
1. Which title tells most about the chapter?
   (A) The North Inlet (B) A Bottle of Wine
   (C) Beaching the *Hispaniola* (D) A Game of Death

REMEMBERING DETAIL
2. Jim spies on Israel Hands and learns that
   (A) Hands has a pistol (B) Hands means to kill him
   (C) Hands already has a bottle of wine (D) the red-capped sailor is really alive
3. Jim realizes he will be safe at least until
   (A) Hands wakes up the next morning (B) Hands has recovered from his wounds (C) he brings Hands the wine (D) the *Hispaniola* has been beached

DRAWING CONCLUSIONS
4. You can tell from the chapter that Israel Hands
   (A) is a deeply religious man (B) is an excellent sailor
   (C) likes Jim very much (D) has never killed anyone before

USING YOUR REASON
5. Jim knows the North Inlet is calm because
   (A) shore bushes are growing on a wrecked ship
   (B) the current is running fast and strong (C) it is long and narrow (D) Hands tells him so

READING FOR DEEPER MEANING
6. Sitting at the top of the mast with a knife in his shoulder, what lesson has Jim learned?
   (A) Trust your shipmates. (B) A cabin boy shouldn't have a gun. (C) Don't be fooled by flattery. (D) A sailor's life is a good life.

THINKING IT OVER
1. How do Jim's quickness and intelligence help him in the battle with Israel Hands?
2. How do chance and luck help Jim in the battle with Israel Hands?

CHAPTER 27

FINDING THE IMPORTANT IDEA
1. This chapter is mostly about
   (A) the moon rising (B) a huge bonfire that Jim sees
   (C) Jim's releasing himself from the mast (D) Jim's
   return across the island

REMEMBERING DETAIL
2. The knife in Jim's shoulder
   (A) is poisoned (B) will not come out (C) has cut him
   very badly (D) has cut him only a little
3. Looking down from the mast, Jim is afraid of
   (A) falling into the water (B) seeing the dead body of
   O'Brien (C) hearing the ghost of Israel Hands
   (D) losing blood from his wound

IDENTIFYING THE MOOD
4. As Jim first steps on shore, he feels
   (A) terrified (B) proud (C) lonely (D) guilty

REMEMBERING DETAIL
5. Whom does Jim find in the fort?
   (A) Israel Hands (B) Ben Gunn (C) The pirates
   (D) Dr. Livesey and Captain Smollett

THINKING IT OVER
1. What do you suppose has happened at the fort while Jim
   has been away?
2. What do you think will happen to Jim now that he is in
   the hands of the pirates?

CHAPTER 28

FINDING THE IMPORTANT IDEA
1. The important idea of the chapter is that
   (A) Jim's friends are missing (B) six pirates are still
   alive (C) Jim makes a bargain with John Silver
   (D) John Silver wants to kill Jim

REMEMBERING DETAIL
2. What does Jim learn about his friends?
   (A) Dr. Livesey is dead. (B) Four of them are still
   alive. (C) Captain Smollett is on John Silver's side.
   (D) Ben Gunn has killed Squire Trelawney.

258

DRAWING CONCLUSIONS

3. You can tell that Captain Smollett believes Jim is
   (A) a traitor (B) dead (C) a gentleman (D) a dutiful
   seaman

USING YOUR REASON

4. When Silver says to Jim, "I'm your last card and you're
   my last card," he means that they
   (A) will both die (B) must depend on each other
   (C) must draw cards to see who will escape (D) will
   eventually have to fight each other

IDENTIFYING THE MOOD

5. At the end of the chapter, John Silver feels
   (A) completely frightened (B) very lucky (C) joyously
   happy (D) almost hopeless

THINKING IT OVER

1. In the middle of the chapter, Jim makes a long speech to
   the pirates. What effect does Jim's speech have on John
   Silver? Does it have the same effect on the pirates?
   Explain.

2. At the end of the chapter, Silver says that Dr. Livesey
   has given him the treasure map. Why might Dr. Livesey
   have done this?

CHAPTER 29

FINDING THE IMPORTANT IDEA

1. The author is mostly interested in telling how
   (A) John Silver regains control of the pirates (B) one of
   the pirates damages his Bible (C) Jim is afraid to go to
   sleep (D) Jim watches the pirates outside the fort

REMEMBERING DETAIL

2. Upon returning to the fort, the pirates tell Silver that
   they have decided to
   (A) kill Jim Hawkins (B) vote him out as captain
   (C) take the map and find the treasure (D) ask Captain
   Smollett to pardon them

3. What does Silver tell the pirates that he will do
   with Jim?
   (A) Make him find the *Hispaniola*   (B) Leave him on
   the island   (C) Use him as a prisoner   (D) Send him as
   a messenger to Dr. Livesey

DRAWING CONCLUSIONS
   4. Silver keeps talking about "damaging the Bible" in order
      to make the pirates
      (A) get angry   (B) laugh   (C) beg for mercy   (D) feel
      afraid

USING YOUR REASON
   5. The pirates are finally persuaded to reelect Silver as
      their captain when they
      (A) see the treasure map   (B) hear Jim's argument
      (C) run out of food   (D) realize the *Hispaniola* is lost

IDENTIFYING THE MOOD
   6. As Jim lies down to sleep, he feels
      (A) calm   (B) relieved   (C) ashamed   (D) troubled

THINKING IT OVER
   1. Before the pirates return to the fort, Silver tells Jim, "I've
      still another card to play." What does this "card" turn out
      to be? How does Silver "play" it?
   2. What does the phrase from the Bible, "Without are dogs
      and murderers" mean to Jim?

CHAPTER 30

FINDING THE IMPORTANT IDEA
   1. Which title tells most about the chapter?
      (A) The *Hispaniola*   (B) Jim's Tears   (C) The Doctor's
      Promise   (D) "Run For It, Jim!"

REMEMBERING DETAIL
   2. Dr. Livesey has come to the fort to
      (A) see Jim Hawkins   (B) give himself up   (C) tend to
      the pirates   (D) bargain with Silver
   3. The pirates have gotten sick because they have
      (A) torn a Bible   (B) slept inside the fort   (C) drunk too
      much rum   (D) camped in a swamp

USING YOUR REASON

4. Following the doctor to the fence, Silver tells Jim to walk slowly because
(A) his good leg hurts (B) otherwise the pirates would be suspicious (C) he doesn't want Jim to fall (D) he has a gun pointed at Jim's head

DRAWING CONCLUSIONS

5. You can conclude from the chapter that Dr. Livesey
(A) knows something about the treasure that's not on the map (B) is willing to let Jim die at the hands of the pirates (C) is lying to Silver when he says he'll try to save him (D) knows that Ben Gunn is dead

READING FOR DEEPER MEANING

6. Jim's behavior in this chapter suggests that one must always
(A) keep one's word (B) trust in luck (C) follow orders (D) help one's enemies

THINKING IT OVER

1. Why doesn't Jim run when he has the chance? What might have happened to Silver had Jim run?
2. What promise does Dr. Livesey make to John Silver? What warning does Dr. Livesey give to John Silver?
3. Dr. Livesey tells Jim that his having found Ben Gunn is "the best deed that ever you did, or will do. . . ." What do you think the doctor means by this?

CHAPTER 31

FINDING THE IMPORTANT IDEA

1. The author is mostly interested in telling how
(A) the pirates talk of Captain Flint (B) Jim saves Silver's life (C) Silver ties a rope around Jim's waist (D) the pirates search for the treasure

REMEMBERING DETAIL

2. According to the map, the chief mark in finding the treasure is
(A) a tall tree (B) a large rock (C) Mizzenmast Hill (D) the river mouth

3. Silver realizes that the human skeleton
   (A) has no skull (B) is that of Captain Flint (C) is pointed in the direction of the treasure (D) is meant to fool them

DRAWING CONCLUSIONS
4. You can tell that after finding the skeleton, the pirates
   (A) fear Flint's ghost (B) are ready to kill Silver
   (C) don't care about the treasure (D) are happy to be nearer the treasure

USING YOUR REASON
5. What strikes John Silver as most illogical?
   (A) That the skeleton is perfectly straight (B) That there is nothing left of the skeleton but clothing
   (C) That the skeleton's hair was yellow (D) That the skeleton is that of a man named Allardyce

THINKING IT OVER
1. Explain the "double game" that Silver is playing.
2. How would you feel if you had found that skeleton? Would you have reacted more like Silver or more like the rest of the pirates?

CHAPTER 32

FINDING THE BEST TITLE
1. Which title tells most about the chapter?
   (A) The Scared Pirates (B) The Three Tall Trees
   (C) Flint's Last Words (D) The Spoiled Bible

REMEMBERING DETAIL
2. The pirates realize that the voice in the trees belongs to
   (A) Squire Trelawney (B) Captain Smollett (C) Ben Gunn (D) Captain Flint
3. What do the pirates discover at the place of the treasure?
   (A) Two more skeletons (B) Ben Gunn's head
   (C) Captain Flint's pistol (D) A hole but no treasure

IDENTIFYING THE MOOD
4. How do the pirates feel when they realize to whom the voice really belongs?
   (A) Angry (B) Sad (C) More frightened (D) Less frightened

262

DRAWING CONCLUSIONS

5. You can tell that if Silver finds the treasure,
   (A) Jim will have little chance of staying alive (B) Jim will get a good share of it (C) he'll kill all the other pirates (D) he'll try to win Dr. Livesey's friendship

USING YOUR REASON

6. Silver reasons that the voice in the trees is not a spirit because
   (A) spirits don't sing (B) spirits don't have shadows (C) the voice is speaking in English (D) the voice has an echo

THINKING IT OVER

1. Where do you think the treasure is? Note that Jim says the hole was "made some time ago." What clue does this give you as to who has found the treasure?

CHAPTER 33

FINDING THE BEST TITLE

1. Which title tells most about the chapter?
   (A) The Cave (B) A Two-Guinea Piece (C) The Death of Merry (D) Victory Over the Pirates

REMEMBERING DETAILS

2. When Silver realizes the treasure is gone, what does he give to Jim?
   (A) A knife (B) A handshake (C) A pistol (D) A two-guinea piece
3. Where is the treasure?
   (A) On Spyglass Hill (B) On Skeleton Island (C) In Ben Gunn's cave (D) Under the tall tree
4. What has happened to the *Hispaniola*?
   (A) The tide has lifted it. (B) It has finally sunk.
   (C) Its mast has burned. (D) The three escaped pirates have boarded it.

DRAWING CONCLUSIONS

5. You can tell that Dr. Livesey would not care if
   (A) Captain Smollett had died (B) Jim had been hurt
   (C) the *Hispaniola* had sunk (D) Silver had died

READING FOR DEEPER MEANING

6. Dr. Livesey indicates to Jim that it is important to
   (A) face death bravely (B) stand by one's duty
   (C) forgive one's enemies (D) live the life of a sailor

THINKING IT OVER

1. Why won't Squire Trelawney punish John Silver?
2. How is Silver acting at the end of the chapter? What do you think will happen to Silver now?

CHAPTER 34

FINDING THE BEST TITLE

1. Which title tells most about the story?
   (A) Seventeen Dead (B) The End of the Tale (C) Ben Gunn's New Job (D) John Silver's Escape

REMEMBERING DETAIL

2. Dr. Livesey doesn't go to help the three pirates because
   (A) Silver says they would kill him (B) he doesn't know where they are (C) he wants them to die (D) Captain Smollett tells him not to
3. What happens to the three pirates?
   (A) They die of fever. (B) They escape to Spanish America. (C) They reach Bristol with John Silver.
   (D) They are left on the island.
4. How many of the *Hispaniola*'s original crew return to Bristol?
   (A) Two (B) Three (C) Five (D) Seventeen

IDENTIFYING THE MOOD

5. Jim's memories of Treasure Island will always be
   (A) happy (B) sad (C) fearful (D) proud

THINKING IT OVER

1. What does Jim mean when he says "Silver's chances of comfort in another world are very small?"
2. Why do you suppose the author does not definitely tell what has happened to John Silver?
3. Are you satisfied with the way the book ends? Why or why not?